MOORE RUBLE YUDELL

H O U S E S & H O U S I N G

MOORE RUBLE YUDELL

H O U S E S & H O U S I N G

Edited and Designed by
Oscar Riera Ojeda
Lucas H. Guerra

Project Assistant
James Mary O'Connor

The American Institute of Architects Press
Washington D.C.

First published in the United States of America by:
Rockport Publishers, Inc.
146 Granite Street
Rockport, Massachusetts 01966
Telephone: (508) 546-9590
Fax: (508) 546-7141
Telex: 5106019284 ROCKORT PUB

Distributed to the book trade and art trade
in the U. S. and Canada by:
The American Institute of Architects Press
1735 New York Avenue NW
Washington, DC 20006
Telephone: (800) 365-2724

Distributed in Mexico, Central and South America by:
Librería Técnica CP67 SA
Florida 683, Local 18 1375 Buenos Aires, Argentina
Telephone: (541) 393-6303 / 394-3947
Fax: (541) 325-7135

Distributed in Spain by:
A ASPPAN SL
Dr. Ramos Castroviejo 63, Local 28035 Madrid, Spain
Telephone: (91) 373-3478 / 373-3613
Fax: (91) 373-7439 / 741-3003

Other distribution by Rockport Publishers, Inc.
Rockport, Massachusetts 01966

ISBN 1-55835-122-1

10 9 8 7 6 5 4 3 2 1

Book Design Concept, Cover Design and Book Layout:
Lucas H. Guerra/Oscar Riera Ojeda
Connexus Visual Communications/Boston, MA
Telephone: (617) 437-7813

Production Manager: Barbara States
Production Assistant: Pat O'Maley
Senior Editor: Rosalie Grattaroti

Printed in Hong Kong

Page 1: Rodes House, California. Page 2: Tegel Villa, Berlin.
Page 6 and 192: Kobe Nishiokamoto Housing, Kobe.
All Photographs by Timothy Hursley

Contents

Dedication

To you Lord
and to all those
who had confidence in me.
A special thanks to my mother, Luisa Testone,
to my sister, Sandra Riera Ojeda,
to Father Ricardo Robira,
and to Laura Fabijanic
who day by day,
gave me constant inspiration.

Oscar Riera Ojeda

In memory of my grandfather,
Hugo Gómez Portillo,
and especially to my mother,
Nora Elsa Gómez,
although very distant,
I always feel close.

Lucas H. Guerra

A *Higher Sense of Appropriateness and Participation*

by Oscar Riera Ojeda

A house, a group of houses or an entire city of them, is a conglomeration of diverse dreams and realities, not always definable or even classifiable, no matter the angle from which it is approached.

Who can tell us for sure what our dwelling space should offer us? What should it represent and signify? What needs should it satisfy? How should a space be designed to offer its inhabitants a physical environment that reaches their highest aspirations, for the best quality of life? What are the parameters and paradigms to be followed in order to find the answers to this controversial and ever-present topic?

These are some of the questions that have been asked, and will continue to be asked, regarding housing issues. Many characteristics and aspects of residential design have remained constant throughout the years, revealing their functionality against many different needs.

Architects, urban designers, and planners have created new and innovative solutions to these questions, but the failure of many, in housing complexes and cities where desolation and violence have become an everyday reality, indicates that there are no "magic solutions."

In this not-so-encouraging panorama of the uninterrupted and decisive struggle behind the difficult task of resolving the problems of residential design — individual and collective — we find the work of the firm Moore Ruble Yudell. From its inception in the late 1970's, when their commissions consisted of simple individual houses, to the present, where large housing projects represent the bulk of their work, their professional practice has been marked by a pro-collaborative architecture, conscious of the housing issues which transcend the disciplinary tools of architecture. Far from elitist, their belief has always been a tight and assiduous participation between all the forces and entities involved in these projects from their very beginning to far beyond their completion. This sense of "group design," based in reality and keeping in mind the social implications, has been the fundamental tool which has guaranteed the acceptance of every one of their projects. This is verified not only in the growing list of clients and the praise of the critics, but in the satisfaction of people who actually live in their buildings.

The search for a greater sense of appropriateness is another characteristic that marks the work of these three architects. This 'appropriateness' strengthens the individual and also our collective identities; one that reaffirms the importance of a sense of belonging and one that takes possession of the landscape and its historical and cultural values. By generating a strong notion of settlement that transcends the private doors to the domain of the public, Moore Ruble Yudell has tried to awaken in the inhabitants of their dwellings, the desire for a stronger and deeper bond with the site and the project. This higher sense of appropriateness and participation, links an architecture in which constructive simplicity balances intellectuality with a practical logic.

A year ago when a Spanish-Argentine publishing house asked me to compile the residential work of this California office for publication in one of its architectural magazines, I never thought it would result in a book. During the course of one year, we have taken on the task of selecting and shaping the presentation of the firm's most significant works. The book, we think, is faithful to the firm and useful and pleasurable to architects and non-architects alike.

I wish to express in conjunction with my partner, Lucas Hugo Guerra, our gratitude to the partners of Moore Ruble Yudell and to James Mary O'Connor, one of the firm's principal associate architects, for entrusting this important and exciting work of design and compilation to us.

The material that follows shows some the most outstanding residential work built in recent years. This qualified assessment is based not only in its mature aesthetic and theoretical underpinnings, but on its fidelity and responsibility to the communities in which they are built. Charles W. Moore, John Ruble and Buzz Yudell are committed to creating places that not only function and shelter but inspire a life of happiness and comfort.

Dualities of Habitation

Charles W. Moore, John Ruble, Buzz Yudell

We began our office some sixteen years ago in much the same way that we currently work: it was an evolutionary process. We had collaborated on several projects in previous years and found that we shared pleasure in the creative act as one of collaboration. We found, as well, that we shared significant concerns about the nature and meaning of our work. As we look back we find themes and continuities both in our manner of work and in the places we ultimately make.

Collaboration: Structure and Freedom

We have always sought the pleasures of a loose informal and highly collaborative way of working: one that balances the collective energy of shared ideas with the contributions of individual initiatives. This is neither the competitive environment of the individual struggling to dominate nor the careful stepwise building of consensus. Rather, it is the interaction and overlay of individual ideas within the context of shared beliefs, goals and mutual respect.

Perhaps the closest analogy is that of the jazz ensemble. Here a small group of musicians shares a common theme, melody and approach to their art. Yet the process is informal and evolutionary enough to encourage, indeed to be dependent upon, individual expression within this communal context. With a general sense of where they're headed, musicians take turns in the lead, interact and improvise as they proceed, and stimulate each other in a balance between individual expression and a common creation.

Without a basis of shared beliefs and inclinations there would not be the energy of collaboration. Without the opportunity for individual exploration there would not be the possibility of discovery and evolution within the ensemble.

Throughout our years of practice together we have explored ways of expanding the circle of collaboration. Within the office this has included associates and project teams working within the context of this team. In a more unusual fashion we have experimented with ways of bringing a community of clients into the process of design. Many of our projects have involved client participation in planning and design workshops.

Just as our way of working is dependent on a balance or resolution of overlapping issues and ideas, so the themes of our work are often dependent on the resolution of opposing tensions or the synthesis of dualities.

Continuity and Change

We see ourselves as deeply rooted and connected to culture, places and people. Architecture is part of a continuum. People have been building roofs over their head and digging holes in the ground for several thousand years. There are aspects of this process of making habitation which occur throughout millennia and through which people feel deeply rooted to their place and secure enough to move out from these centers to explore the rest of the world. The philosopher Karsten Harries has spoken of the "ethical" meaning of architecture. His use of ethical comes from "ethos" by which he means the spirit of the place. We feel that people and communities need and seek a sense of connection to their land, place and culture. The yearnings they have are profound, should not be trivialized, and can contribute through their sense of their own needs and ideas to the architect's effort in place making.

At the same time, dwelling and growing involves chance, exploration and evolution. So, too, should the architecture that is shelter and venue for these actions.

Historicism has become a bête noir because of the arbitrary adoption of historical forms or styles. For us the issue is not one of stylistic devices. We are not interested in historicism per se. We are concerned about connecting to the continuum of ways in which people have, over time, created their houses, markets, places of worship, places of study and institutions.

Popular and Profound

Connections to popular culture can complement and coexist with poetic and profound experiences. Often familiar elements can serve as invitations to participate in the places we make. Commonly understood signs and symbols of the culture can connect us to shared understandings and experiences of our communities. The gabled roof forms of "house" and the central fireplace as "hearth" are resonant of the experience of dwelling. They are popular signs and as such can open a path to interaction with the deeper experiences as architecture engages the senses, intellect and spirit. Poetry is made of language that everyone knows, used in ways that challenge and refresh our understanding of the world. The common elements of architecture can be combined in space, light, time, culture, and the environment to pose new questions and new experiences. The popular and the profound can reinvigorate each other.

Familiar and Surprise

These beliefs have often led us to mix familiar and surprise. The familiar forms make a connection to the place, its culture and history, and also create an environment in which the inhabitants can feel welcomed, engaged and connected. The surprise elements can then begin to stimulate, challenge and pose questions about the very place and culture in which we find ourselves. In the Tegel Harbor Housing, for example, certain forms that are traditional of "house" become the basis of the composition. Yet these forms are not left static or uninflected. The elements are collected and composed sometimes with calm symmetry and sometimes with complex, almost chaotic geometries. At times it is soothing, at other times an expression of many individual identities: the whole is symbolic of the balance between the community and the individual.

At the University of Oregon our science buildings "fit in" to recall the historic patterns of buildings enfronting the main street while creating courtyards between themselves. The scale, color, materials and certain aspects of composition make connections with the older buildings of the campus. Yet surprise and change is around nearly every corner. The community is invited into participation with the buildings by their familiarity and challenged by surprise and variations of the elements.

Order and Chaos

All of our buildings grow in some tension between a clear order and the inclination towards complexity, fragmentation and chaos. Typically individual elements such as the order of the plan, or the order of the section are rather straightforward and clear. It is often the superimposition of multiple parts that generates a complexity or apparent disorder.

At St. Matthew's Church the order of a cross axial plan meets the order of a semi-circular configuration for worship. The cross axial plan is expressed three dimensionally in roof and structural shapes. The centripetal order of worship is expressed in the low, sloping hip roof. It is in the intersection of these parts that a burst of spatial complexity is experienced inside the building, providing many opportunities in the expression of the structure and the play of light as it moves through these intersection orders. While we seek conceptual clarity, we are not often interested in those orders based on minimalism or reductionism in which the alignment of a minimal number of elements becomes a major compositional goal. We admire the inclusivist complexity of Aalto more than the reductionist clarity of Mies.

The action involved in these pursuits is not unlike the art of Bonsai: a clear diagram is carefully "grown," that is, derived analytically from the site, program and the pragmatics of construction. This pattern is then clipped, twisted, interrupted and shaped. If a form is too solid it·is carved, if too tall it is stepped back, if too long, it is bent.

Inside and Out

One aspect of the concern with familiar and surprise is mirrored in the contrast between inside and out. It is often the case that the outsides of our building are more polite, more carefully fitted to their place, and more familiar, than the inside. We take some pleasure in the image of the geode in which the world inside is replete with this surprise of multiple reticulations and complex spatial experiences. The outside, taking its place as a member of a larger community, is often better served by quieter, familiar connections. At the University of Oregon the major center and meeting place for the Science Department is the Physics Atrium, a complex, soaring interior whose shape is largely a resultant of the multiple forces of adjacent buildings. The careful manipulation of light, various balconies and windows further elaborates this as a place to gather, encourage community and allow for discovery.

At the Crossroads School an almost tough, understated exterior quietly fits within a light industrial neighborhood, while inside a street slices through the building. The street is, in turn, pierced by the vertical movement of a court-like space. The street and court become stages for the communal life of the school community.

Movement and Stillness

The experiential and choreographic aspect of architecture has been an ongoing concern. Architecture is more than large-scale sculpture. At its essence it involves the creation of places that support and celebrate dwelling and action in all their manifestations. How people fit in, move through and kinesthetically understand their environments is essential to the experience of architecture. Movement and stillness are equally important. One suggests action, the other suggests thought or regeneration. Our buildings should be able to encourage and allow a full range of choreographic experiences within them. We are interested in an architecture which is humanistic and body centered, rather than one whose paradigm is the machine. We want the relation between our buildings and their inhabitants to be complex and inviting but never coercive and overbearing.

People should feel supported and encouraged to dwell in and explore their places.

Dwelling in Space and Light

Ultimately architecture makes places for dwelling: whether for the individual, the family or the whole community. Certain archetypal qualities of architecture such as proportions of space and qualities of light can and should be allies in the making of places for dwelling. We feel great admiration for architects as diverse in time as Palladio and Kahn for the ways in which they manipulate proportions of space and qualities of light and shadow, raising these to the level of poetics. In this area, as well, we often find ourselves manipulating contrasting elements. We enjoy the surprise of moving from tight quiet spaces to grandly energetic ones. We've admired Junichiro Tanizaki's book "In Praise of Shadows" for its encouragement of the appreciation of darkness and shadow as places of discovery, mystery and quiet. He chafes at the modern world's inability to accept anything but the harsh clarity of strong clear light. The contrast and complexity of the range from bright through dappled light to dusk and darkness is one more realm in which life and thought can be enriched.

Applied and Integral Color

A logical extension of the interest in light is the use of color. As advanced by Tina Beebe, color and ideas about color have become a critical dimension in all of our work. In the Rodes House, our first built work together, abstract, applied color is carefully used to delineate the proportions of the double-cube living room, and create tonal sequences leading from one space to the next — at times deep and secluded, at other times a burst of brightness turning a solid wall into pure light. Later, at St. Matthew's Church, we began to introduce equal amounts of painted and natural color: painted steel and plaster played with and against Douglas fir, clay tile and granite. Here the use of applied color serves to clarify — cool (green) on the outside, warm (rose) on the inside — giving a diagrammatic order to this richly figurative building. It is this conceptual overlay — and not always such a simple one — which makes applied colors so essential for us. Simultaneously abstract and sensual, this is one of the most evidently "modern" aspects of our work.

Ornament and Abstraction

If there is any area with which we struggle as a group, it is the broad range of choices on the scale of the tough and abstract to the warmly elaborated. One is tempted to read this scale "modern vs. traditional," but we like to think that all our work incorporates tradition by reference: the specifics are carefully recast, whether at the scale of a campus plan or a window detail. Conversely, we hope that our use of abstraction functions as it did in Wright's early career: recognizable forms and elements are put through extraordinary shifts in scale, proportion and position. Some works, such as the Rodes House, the Yudell/Beebe House, and the grand stair at the St. Louis Art Museum, are pared down to essential, taut forms and surfaces which are enriched by material and color. Elsewhere, most notably St. Matthew's Church and the University of Oregon, interiors and exteriors are richly embroidered, in seemingly traditional ways. But tradition is elusive and suggestive, especially in the details.

We tend to understand ornament as Kent Bloomer has long argued for it: the careful detailed elaboration of a larger system or order, adding layers of meaning. At St. Matthew's Church the inspiration was Ruskinian and the result is a kind of visual acoustics. Applied wood battens on plaster walls create a harmonic background for larger sculptural elements such as the triumphal arches, which are all dressed up for liturgical celebration.

Ornament also serves to highlight a program of human activity — a kind of literary overlay as is suggested by Charles Jencks. At St. Matthew's wall sconces illuminate the seven gifts of the Holy Spirit. Kent Bloomer's own metal sculpture in the Physics Atrium at the University of Oregon offers a representation of energy states from its solid base, up to the top of the stairs, where hundreds of reflective leaves whip the space and light into a swirling shower of pure sparkle: an artist's homage to cloud neblae.

As designs evolve, we often diverge on the question of how elaborately detailed we want the work to be. At this point it would be hard to say whether either tendency will be ascendant in our future work. We hope we will always be strongly influenced by the specifics of site, programs and client committees, and thereby produce buildings and places which, however abstract or figurative, are a pleasure to discover.

Dwelling in the Land

Perhaps the first and most critical decision for most buildings is their siting, placement and fit within the land. Here again we don't see our buildings as machines or sculptures set on pristine lawns or plazas but rather almost as trees rooted in their place and growing upwards and outwards in response to various environmental influences. Living and working in California has heightened our sense that buildings are the starting point for dwelling in a habitable landscape. Consequently, much of our work involves shaping the spaces between buildings as carefully as the buildings themselves are shaped. In our new Cultural Center for Escondido, California, four buildings are not only shaped themselves, but in turn shape some twelve courtyards of various scales sized for a range of intimate to grand community activities.

In many of our houses this sequence of movement through courtyards, to cultivated gardens and beyond to native landscape become as important as the sequences of movement and experience within the house. In our housing project in Kobe the impetus for the shaping of the project came from a sense of connecting to the original landscape: we reinforced the important linkage of the site between the mountains and the ocean, restored a sense of the original topography, and designed the buildings in relation to a sequence of landscape experiences. The buildings were shaped much like ranges of mountains arrayed around a valley. This became a way for us to feel a profound connection to the place even though as foreign architects we felt we should not and could not try to make buildings which themselves seemed Japanese. Our connection was rather about a more fundamental relationship to the place and land. We were later gratified to learn that Professor Higuchi in a recent book has argued that the archetypal pattern of settlement for Japan once was buildings arrayed like ranges of hills around meadows and streams.

Evolution

It is within the realm of these many overlapping influences, stimulated by the tension of opposites, that we take pleasure in working. We seek ways of maintaining continuity and connection to places, culture and inhabitants of our buildings. We simultaneously seek to challenge and surprise and to explore new ways of making places. Our work is a partnership among ourselves and with and for people who will use and experience it. Our process is one of evolution: guided by common understandings, commitments and principles, but inflected and influenced by exploration, surprise and chance.

Top Left: Renovations to the West Wing
Decorative Arts Galleries, St. Louis Art Museum
St. Louis, Missouri
Photograph by Timothy Hursley

Top Right: The Peter Boxenbaum Arts Education Center
Crossroads School, Santa Monica, California
Photograph by Timothy Hursley

Bottom: St. Matthew's Episcopal Church
Pacific Palisades, California
Photograph by Timothy Hursley

Designing the Act of Dwelling

Charles W. Moore

A dwelling should be the center of the universe for the people who share it. To puzzle out a shape for the center of the universe with one interested family is a complex task, full of particular sensibilities, personal tastes, and specific requirements, not to mention budgets. But to place dozens, or even hundreds of these centers together, for inhabitation by people whose identities are generally not even known to the designer and in constant flux approaches the hopeless. Much of our practice has been in this tenuous realm, trying to discover the extent to which physical shapes and spaces can impart a sense of place, and trying to develop a framework in which the inhabitants provide (as we believe they must) most of the energy for the act of dwelling.

The need is for inhabitation, public and private, marking places where people as members of the body public as well as individuals can take over some piece of public space. It is the great failure of too many of our "public" spaces (like the public areas in housing projects) that they are uninhabited and uninhabitable, by our bodies or our minds, or by those allies in habitation, flowers and statues and especially light which could help us make our world our own. A generation ago architects expected megastructures to bring a new scale to urban building. Now, a look at the Sunday real estate pages will reveal only some ads for homes in megastructures, but plenty for their opposite, the village: condominium villages, vacation villages, shopping villages (offices come in "parks") and even, in Kerrville, Texas, a "junk village."

One of my most successful attempts at making a series of places, a simple village, inhabitable by many people, was ten condominiums at the Sea Ranch. With my partners, Donlyn Lyndon, Bill Turnbull and Dick Whitaker, we were able to invest enough of our pooled energy early on, so the building was able to come to life, even before its inhabitants began to live there. Our problem was to make a condominium consisting of ten units on a dramatic cliff overlooking the Pacific. Relentless winds sweeping in from the sea required that we slope most of the roofs toward the wind, keep the volumes simple in honor of the vernacular barns and use the mass of buildings to shield two inner courtyards. For the interiors, we relied on formal ideas that we had been developing for our houses: the four-postered aedicula paired with a miniature house with an encompassing room, and sheltered them with a sturdy heavy-timbered barn-like structure, very carefully shaped to cope with the winds and weather. It feels to us, twenty-five years later, inhabitable and satisfying still.

The villages we all long for offered their inhabitants, according to J.B. Jackson, five benefits: security, privacy, sociability, justice and a place connected to the ancestral dead. But our new villages cannot simply duplicate the old ones, since most of us are not at all anxious for the old restrictions. Since most of us in the twentieth century (with its ease of travel and electronic extension) have wandered far from our ancestors' graves, we are left to rely on the more general gift of memory, which with the other boons, security, privacy, sociability, we then somehow transfigure into the villages of our own time. Most important of all, the village offers validation — everyone has a place to call their own, a place to feel centered (in the way that ballet dancers do) in a particular place in our increasingly complex but homogenous world. With the city, on the other hand, comes the specter of anomie, the person alone in the world. We've found that if we load even a corner, district, or suburb of the city with sympathetic people, these parts can function as a village, like Greenwich Village, or Castro Street or a settlement at the Country Club, or a tennis village.

Can a physical place help satisfy our longing for the validation of the village? Architects and planners have to think so. We must learn to fashion edges (to promote security), centers (to promote sociability), organization (to promote discernible order, imply justice and promote privacy) and icon and ornament (to induce and connect us to our culture).

For all the non-dialectic, I am opposed to some forces at work on our buildings: I am against attitudes that make buildings, with their capacity to speak, churlish or mute. I am against the rapid homogenization of place. I believe that silence is imposed by doing buildings without care, and multiplying that carelessness without concern. The result has been that buildings, when rendered speechless, have become so uninteresting that the public, the inhabitants at large, have just stopped listening or caring. The most difficult problem of architects in our society, I believe, is to learn how to spread our attention, over 40 or 400 or 4,000 dwellings, say, instead of just one or four, without spreading our attention so thin that it becomes ineffective. Many architects do pretty good single family houses, and it's possible to join the energies of the owners or inhabitants of the house to those of the architect and builder and all the other people involved to create a place sufficiently full of energy to stand a good chance of repaying that energy to the inhabitants, which is what I think a good house does. But when an architect is asked to do 400 or 4,000 houses at the same time, it doesn't work just to divide the investment of energy 400 or 4,000 ways. The energy investment quickly sinks well below the point where the energies of the inhabitants can be attracted, or where the energies in the dwellings are sufficient to repay concern; so the architect must invent other strategies for investing his energy so that the buildings can become inhabitable and feel like the center of the universe.

HOUSES

Houses: Shelter, Dreams, and Community

Buzz Yudell

From the inception of our office the design of houses has been central to our interests and pleasure. For us architecture is giving form to habitation and the house is the primal representation of this process. A house embodies perhaps the most intimate relationship between humans and architecture. It reaches beyond shelter to express the needs and dreams of its inhabitants, and it helps to define and mediate a relationship to the landscape and the greater community.

A house is not only the shelter and manifestation of an individual or family, it is, as well, one quantum in the making of community. The challenges of designing the individual house may differ at some point from those of multiple unit housing, but they share many aspects, as expressions of collective culture and community.

As with all architecture, houses evolve out of a dynamic tension of abstract and idealized principles, synthesized with the needs and dreams of the individuals involved (inhabitants and architects) and the imperatives of the place and culture. The individual house develops out of a more protected and intimate communication between architect and owner. While the house has its role in the public realm, it can be a particularized, at times idiosyncratic, exploration of the character and lives of specific individuals. We take pleasure in making houses that balance archetypal and primal expressions of shelter and domain with specific personal manifestations of character, dreams and place.

In the Rodes house, perhaps the tightest fit with the specific life of the owner, a cool "Palladian" geometry of cubes and double cubes of space underlies a more personal agenda of spatial development. Here a grand formal living space is the focus of the public life of the house, like a plaza in a town. On a tight budget the owner and architect opted to play this grandness against intimate spaces in the surrounding "poché."

The connection to landscape and climate is always of generative importance in our initial explorations. If our housing deals with graded hierarchies of public to private realms, our houses put equal emphasis on the rooms inside, "rooms" outside and transitional spaces such as porches, loggias and terraces. Working in California has increased our concern for this spectrum of places but these principles apply, with adaptation, in all climates.

The Yudell/Beebe house takes it site organization from the north–south mountain–sea axis and the east–west relation to the stream and landscape. A family of courts and pergolas make habitable rooms, responding to varying views and sun orientations. They also create transitions from life inside to the natural landscape.

At the Schetter house, a large plan is given order and diversity by its organization of interior spaces which interlock with 12 exterior courtyards of diverse character. These garden rooms vary from a "secret garden" off the library, to a linear promenade marking the edge where the house meets the horizon.

The spaces within can celebrate life and activities of many characters and dimensions. While we employ geometry and proportion to create spatial sequences and order, the power of the house resides in its potential to accommodate and stimulate a great range of human potential and emotion.

We increasingly seek a quiet complexity in which the architecture does not overwhelm life within, yet is still rich enough to surprise and delight. Rooms have the power, by their containment, proportion and material, to stimulate and enable human activity. They can provide stillness or exuberance, intimacy or grandeur. We welcome this archetypal power of the room as a vessel. At the same time, the dynamic potential of interpenetrating fluid space can contrast and collide with a more formally defined space.

In the Kwee house, the formality of family life is expressed in the proportions and axes of the living room, dining room and library, while master and children's bedrooms are disposed around an irregular and informal garden. In 647 Marine Street a tiny space is given ambiguity and mystery of scale by the sweep of an arc from inside to out and by the visual connection of small places through layers of space. The Quarry Road house threads several partially defined rectangular spaces along the path of a great ellipse.

Walls come to life as they have logic, clarity and purpose in the plans. In the Anawalt House a series of gently radiating walls define layers of rooms and courtyards and splay open toward the sea. At times they are thick enough to inhabit. The Yudell/Beebe House layers parallel walls in a gradient from closed to open, finally "dematerializing" into open pavilions as rooms in nature. The walls of the Kwee House trace a strong pattern of overlapping rectangles which define a plaid geometry of habitation.

The sequences of places adds meaning to them as well as experiential and kinesthetic richness. We understand the world by orienting and moving our bodies and minds through it. The interaction between our movement and our environment is a profound choreographic dialogue.

The Walrod House links rooms to each other and the house to the land by virtue of a sensuous "garden to sky" path of movement. This occurs in complementary fashion both inside the house and without. The interior path is animated by transitions in height, width, qualities of light, view and speed of movement. Its dynamic quality contrasts and compliments the defined quiet of the "rooms." Here, and in other houses, the movement spaces are not simply circulation but allow for libraries, dining and lounge areas.

In the Inman House the formality of living and dining rooms is complemented by the sweep of curved circulation that links the house to a garden pavilion from which one descends to nature.

The realms of the mind and spirit are inextricably tied to the physicality of architecture. In "The Poetics of Space," Gaston Bachelard speaks eloquently of the resonance of archetypal places within the house. Thus the attic and basement are charged with specific meanings. To be underground or in the sky is psychically differentiated from a ground level habitation. The festive roof pavilion in the Superba House, and the animated path to it, celebrate the connection between house and sky. The earth to sky progression in the Walrod House creates a narrative connection of these domains.

Memory exists simultaneously with present experience. The past and present inform each other with kaleidoscopic complexity. Charles has made each of his own houses, in part, as treasuries of momementi: from the pyramid as cosmic container of toys, trains and soldiers in Centerbrook to the polychrome elliptical wall of Kachina totems and talismen in Austin. These places both record a life of wonder and, by their collective presence, stimulate the mind and creative spirit.

The pleasures that we've taken from making houses that express their inhabitants, place and culture have, as well, informed our aspirations for housing and urban planning. While scale, location and culture may vary, the basic needs and satisfactions of dwelling unite us across time and space.

Top: Villa Superba Dining Room
Venice, California
Photograph by Timothy Hursley

Bottom: Anawalt House Living Room
Malibu, California
Photograph by Jane Lidz

RODES HOUSE
Los Angeles, California

This house was designed for a bachelor English professor who wanted a serene and formal home on a modest budget. The house evolved from the limitations of its site — a flat trapezoid-shaped orchard with hills rising steeply on two sides. The orchard is loose fill and unbuildable and the only way the house could meet its low budget was to span the hill.

This span was first designed with trusses within the exterior walls. It then evolved into a series of three trussed bridges which pierced the long symmetrical curve of the facade, the inner wall of the living room, and the rear of the dining room conservatory. In the final scheme, the truss construction was not affordable and the span was achieved with a buried bridge of caissons and grade beams. But the owner and the architects had taken such pleasure in the play of the straight trusses and the curved facade that it is recollected with a plane of lightweight lattice which invites vegetation and serves as an armature for lighting.

The gourmet owner wanted, in a very small house, generous provisions for cooking and dining, and a grand living room. To save space he was happy to settle for an alcove bed in the pattern of Thomas Jefferson's. Upstairs a guest room and bath are across the bridge from a small study. On a tight budget the strategy involved keeping two grand rooms (living and dining) and treating the modesty of bedroom, study and guest room as the positive opportunity to create intimate and special places. The contrast between intimate and grand serves to enhance the character of both.

In front of the house an oval patio serves as a stage for performers visiting the client's university, while guests sit in an orange grove laced with fragments of a terraced amphitheater. Modest material — stucco exteriors and plaster interiors — are animated by pastel walls and vegetation.

For the owner and the architects, special pleasures of this house exist in its responsiveness to both the apparent and hidden qualities of the site.

Project: Rodes House
Size of Lot: 34,100 square feet
Size of Project: 1,850 square feet

Owner: David Rodes
Design Architect: Moore Ruble Yudell
Principal-in-Charge: Buzz Yudell
Principal Architect: Charles Moore
Principal Architect: John Ruble;
Project Team: J. Timothy Felchlin,
Regula Campbell, Jim Meyer
Color: Tina Beebe
Photography: Timothy Hursley

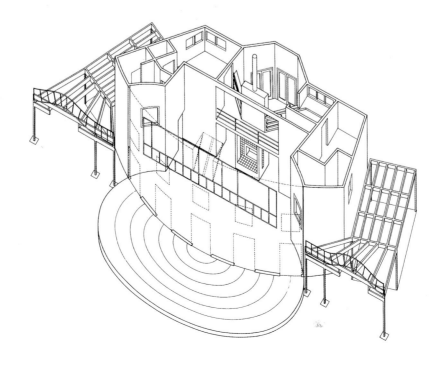

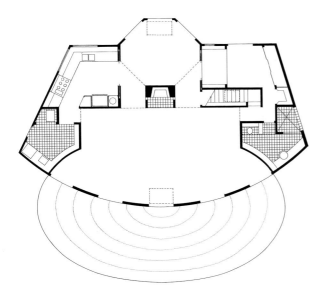

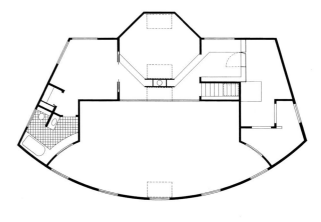

First and Second Floor Plans

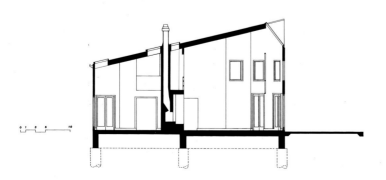

ANAWALT HOUSE

Malibu, California

The clients for this house on a coastal bluff asked for a house based on the tradition of Southern California's Spanish idiom and connected to the dramatic views of Santa Monica Bay. While we admire much of California's Spanish-inspired architecture of the early part of the century, we wished to develop a house that grew out of the underlying organizational and climatic principles of that architecture rather than stylistic characteristics alone. We wanted the house to be evocative of earlier courtyard houses while exploring a freer expression of the architectural elements.

We saw this house as evolving out of the interplay of courts which create tranquil centers, and walls which frame views. Some of the courts are literal, like the parking court and entry court. Others are implied, like the living room and the library, which are configured as large and small courts at the heart of the house. These interior rooms borrow the character of outdoor spaces, while a set of carefully proportioned outside living spaces are as vital as the interior rooms.

The spaces of the house are defined by a set of walls which splay out toward the ocean and step down with the topography. When these walls surround the bigger and more public spaces they are thicker, to give them greater substance and power. They are at times especially solid to read as mass or very pierced, framing views to terraces and the sea. In places they extend free of the body of the house to give a stronger elemental presence. The house fits and moves with the landforms yet stakes its place on the horizon. The massing culminates in a tower that anchors the house on the bluff and provides its own rooftop redoubt protected by thick parapet walls.

Finally, this is a house of courts and walls, familiar and formal, that learns from the best of its traditions while bringing its own freedoms and expressions to its inhabitants and its landscape.

Project: Anawalt House
Size of Lot: 1.5 acres
Size of House: 4,500 square feet enclosed,
6,000 square feet total

Design Architect: Moore Ruble Yudell
Principal-in-Charge,
Principal Architect: Buzz Yudell
Principal Architect: John Ruble
Principal Architect: Charles Moore
Project Architect: Daniel Garness,
Akai Ming-Kae Yang
Color: Tina Beebe
Renderings: Brian Tichenor
Photography: Jane Lidz
Model: Steven Gardner
Model Shots by Craig Currie, Moore
Ruble Yudell Collection

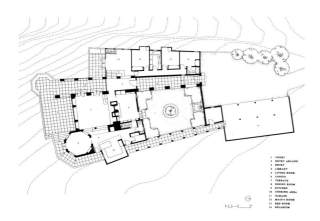

Ground Level Plan

1 COURT
2 ENTRY ARCADE
3 ENTRY
4 LIBRARY
5 LIVING ROOM
6 LOGGIA
7 TERRACE
8 DINING ROOM
9 KITCHEN
10 COOKING AREA
11 GARAGE
12 MAID'S ROOM
13 BED ROOM
14 SOLARIUM

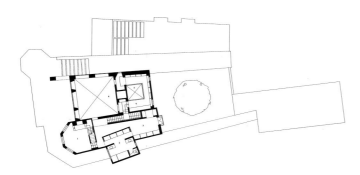

Second Level Plan

1 MASTER BEDROOM
2 MASTER BATH
3 DRESSING ROOM
4 LIBRARY LOFT
5 OPEN TO LIBRARY
6 OPEN TO LIVING ROOM

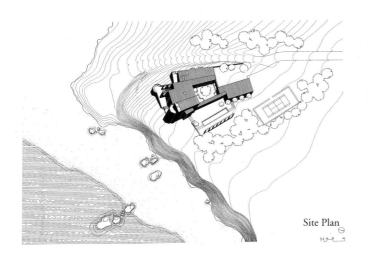

Site Plan

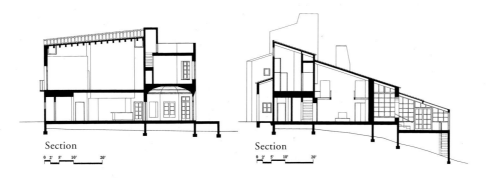

Section

0 2' 5' 10'   20'

Section

0 2' 5' 10'   20'

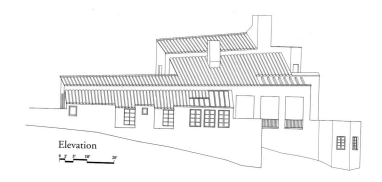

Elevation

0 2' 5' 10'   20'

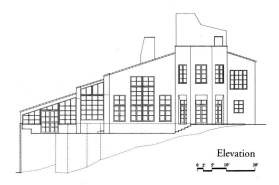

Elevation

INMAN HOUSE
Atlanta, Georgia

Our client's grandparents had built Georgia's most splendid neo-Baroque mansion designed by noted Atlanta architect Carl Schutze in the 1920s, so there was some expectation that the Inman's 3,000 square foot house in Buckhead would evoke a formal grandness well beyond its modest size. This was aided by the site, a great piney hillside overlooking a lovely park and by the Inmans' love of Italian gardens.

The parti is a variation on Charles Moore's entry to the exhibition "Houses for Sale" — an entry hall, on axis with the garden, is flanked by lofty living and dining rooms, and looks down hill toward the great porch, which itself looks into the towering pines.

At the entry front rendered brick walls encircle a cour d'honneur complete with porte-cochère on an otherwise quiet facade. Tall triple-hung windows suggest the nearly Jeffersonian inventiveness which characterizes the interiors. Under a simple hipped roof, the living, dining and kitchen-family rooms make full use of the volume, creating the taller, elegantly proportional rooms for which southern houses are admired, and which make sense in the long Georgian summers. Behind this formal suite, an arc of bedrooms and their gallery sweeps down into the garden and hillside ending at the great porch. The porch recalls one of our clients' favorite places at his grandparents' home and was developed as a high open pavilion at the very center of the house site. Cabinet shops at the Inmans' own lumber company produced triple-hung windows, mahogany doors, and custom wood work, giving special profile and detail to the carefully proportioned interiors.

Project: Inman House
Size of Lot: 23,950 square feet
Size of House: 3,052 square feet

Design Architect: Moore Ruble Yudell
Principal-in-Charge,
Principal Architect: John Ruble
Principal Architect: Charles Moore
Principal Architect: Buzz Yudell
Project Team: James Mary O'Connor,
Peter Zingg, Brian Tichenor
Renderings: James Mary O'Connor
Photography: Timothy Hursley

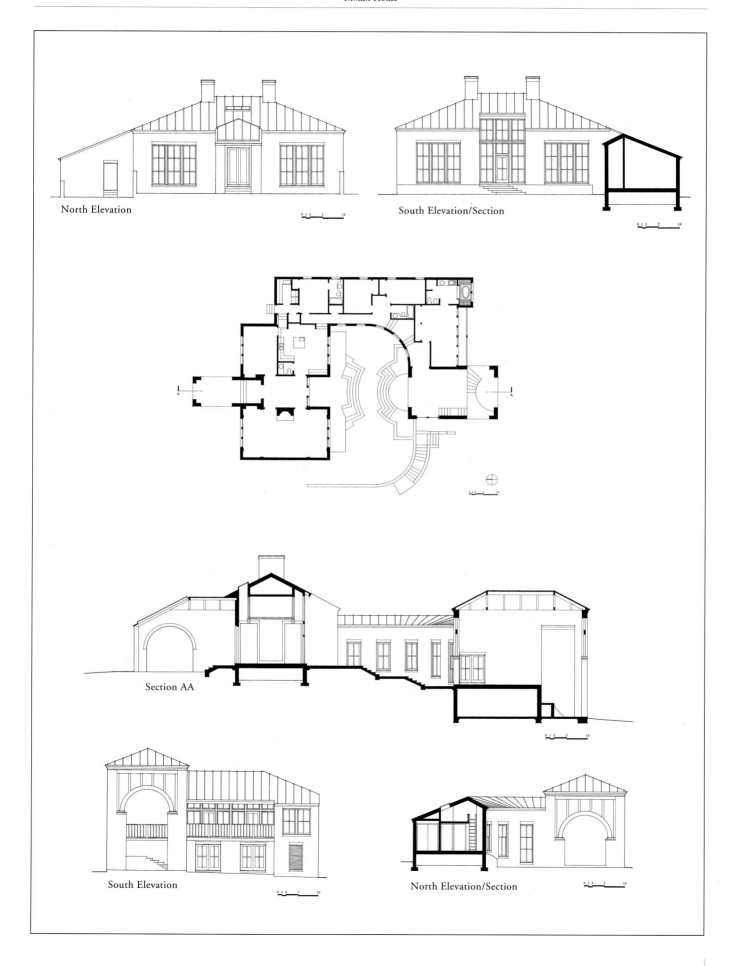

North Elevation

South Elevation/Section

Section AA

South Elevation

North Elevation/Section

MARINE STREET HOUSE
Santa Monica, California

To escape the runaway rent escalation of the late 1970s we teamed up with my partner John Ruble to buy a 50' x 100' lot in the Ocean Park neighborhood of Santa Monica. This lot had two small beach bungalows. The front house was a "fixer-upper" with some redeeming architectural details. The back house was a "tear-down"; a 20' x 29' uninsulated box made of scavenged windows and subdivided into five tiny rooms. John and his wife restored the front house and we took the "shack at the back." The challenge was to transform the shack on a tiny budget.

Every intervention had to do double duty. The house was gutted except for plumbing walls. Three sides of the house (facing side yards and alley) were left untouched and the front facade with a new interior was slipped in like a new drawer. A strong new shape, a partial ellipse, was inserted to define a new central living area. Small adjacent spaces (dining, bedroom/study) communicated through wall openings to give a more ambiguous spatial reading.

A second curving wall is lined with books and gives a study-like quality to the sleeping area. It defines the longest possible dimension and completes itself in a mirror to extend the spatial reading. The wall also contains a "secret" door to the bathroom since a separate vestibule area was not workable in the 580 square foot house.

Much of the house is fitted out like a ship's cabin or Pullman with built-in bed, banquette, study and storage. The ellipse completes itself outside as front steps engaging the entry garden. A second small garden room and new entry is made of the dining area. The geometry of the gardens and house add a sense of expanse to the living spaces.

A new "beach bungalow" facade was composed of windows salvaged from bungalows demolished in the neighborhood. Its more complex exterior color scheme is one of the few clues to the spatial surprises inside the clapboard box.

Project: Marine Street House
Size of Lot: 2,500 square feet
Size of House: 570 square feet

Owner: Buzz Yudell and Tina Beebe
Architect: Buzz Yudell
Landscaping: Tina Beebe
Color: Tina Beebe
Photography: Henry Bowles

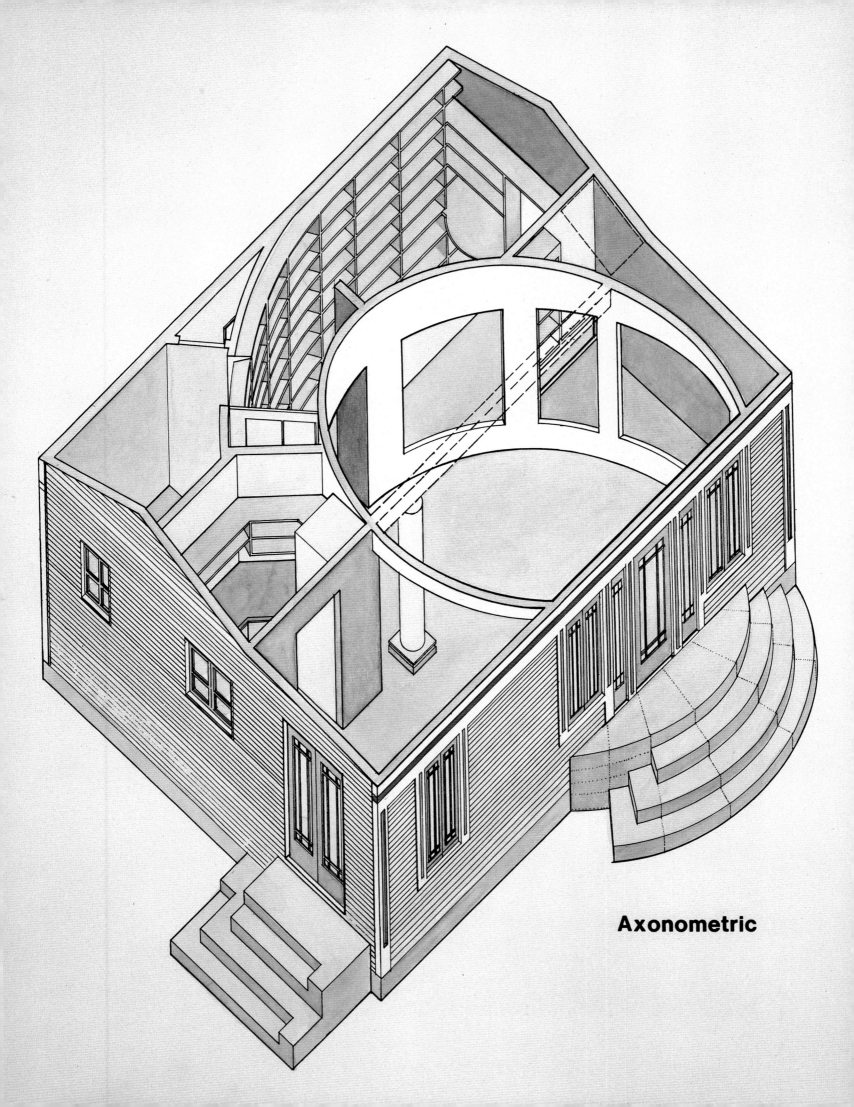

Axonometric

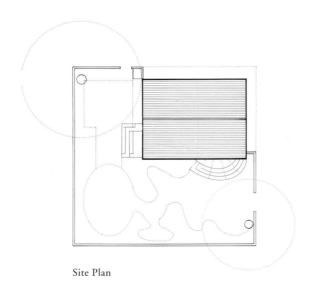

Site Plan

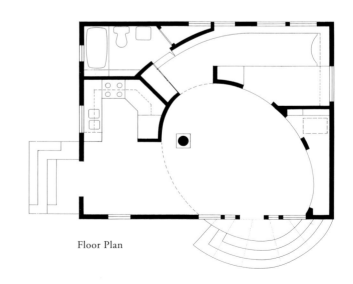

Floor Plan

West Elevation

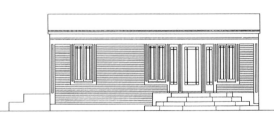

South Elevation

Section Looking East

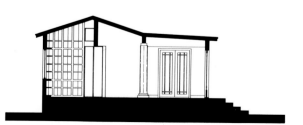

Section Looking West

QUARRY ROAD HOUSE
Austin, Texas

Two houses and two studios comprise the complex at 2102 Quarry Road in Austin which is set within a rolling site filled with large central Texas oak trees. Our challenge was to match our needs for large amounts of studio and living space with the scale and character of the houses and bungalows in the neighborhood, and at the same time, chop down as few of the venerable oak trees as possible. To diminish the scale of the compound, we divided the residential and studio spaces into several small buildings and organized them around a central courtyard and a 47 foot lap pool. Each building has a private entrance, allowing us the freedom to come and go with a semblance of independence. Views from the houses look into the shared court as well as to landscaped gardens and the shady grove of trees beyond. Board and batten walls painted a soft gray and galvanized metal roofs establish a neutral palette characteristic of the neighborhood which also works as a backdrop to the dramatic oak trees on the site.

The courtyard and the interiors of the houses and studios (our private world that is invisible to the neighbors) were the places where we could stir up the magic. In the courtyard, we painted the walls in bright teal and deep blue tones. Rich, green vegetation covers grids of trellis on the walls and an arbor hovering over the swimming pool. The axis of the lap pool (which is dramatically illuminated at night) ends in a Baroque mirror flanked by finials and lanterns. Moving inside the houses the intensity increases. A broad ellipse sweeps through the Moore house, cuts through the Andersson house, and then swings back outside to form the back wall of the courtyard. Moore's section of ellipse is painted in a dizzying array of colors, and is lined with bookshelves crammed with books and folk toys, as well as an enfilade of talismen (borrowed from Karl Friedrich Schinkel) that are painted with patterned shields. In the Andersson house, the elliptical wall takes the shape of the cliff-like dwellings in Benares,

Project: Quarry Road House

Size of Lot: 1.2 acres
Size of Project: 4,130 square feet total (includes one 2,400 square foot house with two bedrooms, living room, dining room, library; one 900 square foot house with a single bedroom and guest room; and two 800 square feet studio spaces.
Year of Commission: 1985
Year of Completion: 1991

Architects: Charles W. Moore, Arthur Andersson
Construction Documents: Richard Dodge
Assistants: Mell Lawrence, Paul Lamb
Special Carpentry: Gary Furman
Photography: Timothy Hursley

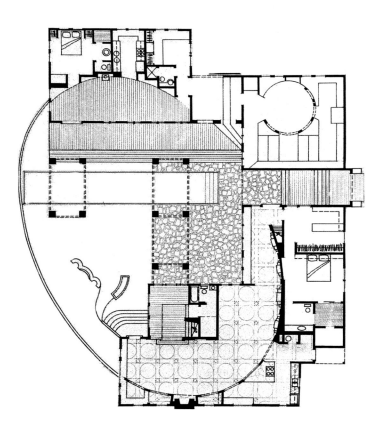

painted in soft grays and whites, and is topped with subtle architectural ornament including a Borrominian door frame, and finally portraits of the founding fathers of Texas. The main architecture studio is populated with an orchard of painted columns that mimic Domenech y Montaner's tile columns in the Catalan Music School but are topped off with our own "order" of Moose antlers.

In the Austin compound, we hoped to make a world where drama and surprise lurk in moving from outside to inside through a changing set of images, from subdued to exuberant, as well as those feelings associated with arrival and repose — the act of having gotten somewhere.

Section Through Courtyard Looking West

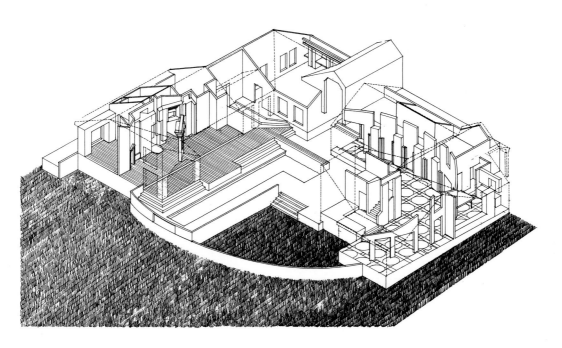

Section Through Courtyard Looking North

SCHETTER HOUSE
Pacific Palisades, California

Working with our clients, a professional couple and their children, we sought to create a house based on an intimate dialogue between building and landscape. This large house is organized around a series of 12 courtyards of diverse character. The courtyards, functioning as a series of outside rooms, became as important as, and complementary to, the rooms within.

Each garden room is specific to its character. A "secret" garden outside the library provides a small contemplative complement to its interior partner. The terrace and loggia near the kitchen and family area provide an outside cooking and dining room to function in tandem with the rooms within. The gardens of the living and dining room area are more formally composed in relation to their counterparts.

The organization of the house on a modified H-shaped plan seeks to modulate its size and scale, developing a range of places of varying formality, size and character.

The life of the family needs to accommodate a range of activities and entertainment from intimate to grand and casual to formal. The house and garden rooms accommodate this diversity. An east–west axis along a gallery moves from more casual family spaces to the formally proportioned library and living rooms. The H-plan allows each piece to function as a "pavilion" with multiple views and ventilation. Strong visual and formal axes link these "pavilions." The choreography of the house is flexible but rich, allowing for many paths of movement. Rooms inside and out provide places of "quiet" as counterpoint to the more dynamic plan and organizing movement. The house scales down toward neighbors, orienting views for maximum privacy and benefit of the borrowed landscape of the Topanga Mountains.

As a whole the house and garden seek to give form to the life of the Schetter family, providing a place at once intimate and grand, full of choice and surprise yet rooted to its landscape.

Project: Schetter House
Size of Lot: 21,075 square feet
Size of Project: 10,000 square feet

Design Architect: Moore Ruble Yudell
Principal-in-Charge,
Principal Architect: Buzz Yudell
Principal Architect: John Ruble
Project Architect: Akai Ming-Kae Yang
Project Team: Neal Matsuno, Tony Tran,
Tony Tam, John Taft, Craig Curie
Landscaping Team: Tina Beebe, Mario
Violich
Color: Tina Beebe
Renderings: Akai Ming-Kae Yang
Photography: Craig Currie, Moore Ruble
Yudell Collection

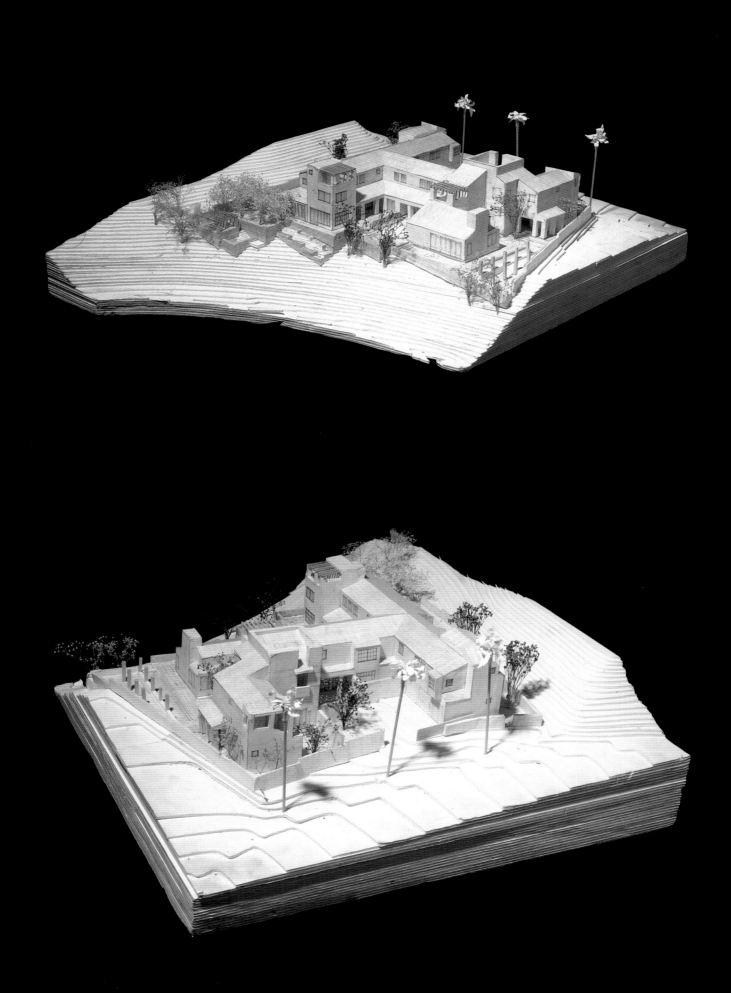

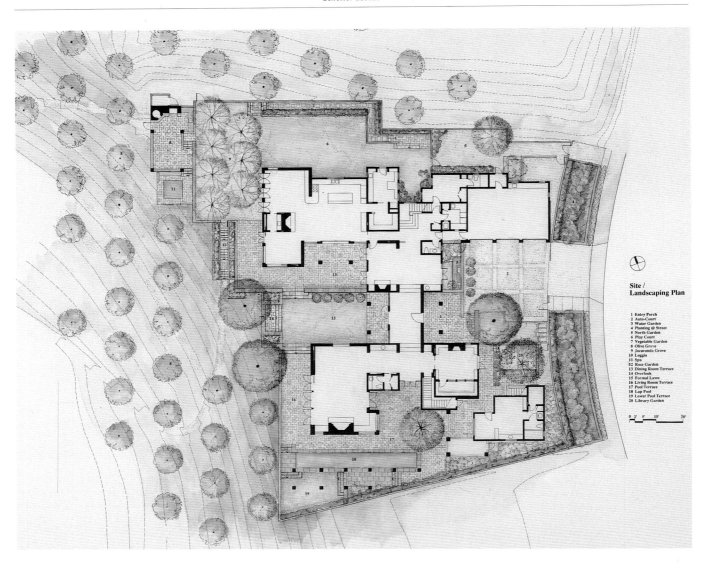

**Site /
Landscaping Plan**

1 Entry Porch
2 Auto-Court
3 Water Garden
4 Planting @ Street
5 North Garden
6 Play Court
7 Vegetable Garden
8 Olive Grove
9 Jacaranda Grove
10 Loggia
11 Spa
12 Rose Garden
13 Dining Room Terrace
14 Overlook
15 Formal Lawn
16 Living Room Terrace
17 Pool Terrace
18 Lap Pool
19 Lower Pool Terrace
20 Library Garden

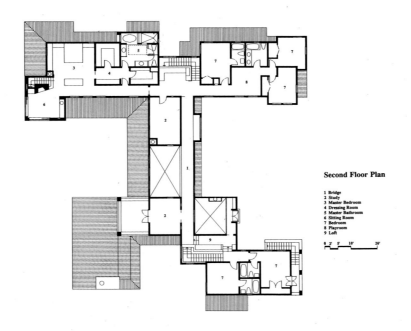

Second Floor Plan

1 Bridge
2 Study
3 Master Bedroom
4 Dressing Room
5 Master Bathroom
6 Sitting Room
7 Bedroom
8 Playroom
9 Loft

YUDELL/BEEBE HOUSE

Malibu, California

Since moving to Southern California we had imagined building a courtyard house in close partnership with the landscape and climate. After some years of searching, the only buildable lot in budget was a hillside lot of 100' x 600' bordered by a dry creek on its west. Setbacks from the stream on one side and Fire Department access required on the other, resulted in a long thin buildable area which had dissuaded other buyers but challenged and intrigued us.

The house evolved from the constraints and pleasures of the site. From east to west the house unfolds as layers of habitation: from carefully proportioned rooms to a sunny gallery broad enough for sitting and dining, to a stepping street onto a set of pergolas that function as garden rooms of varying character, then to cultivated gardens and finally to the streambed and uncultivated chaparral.

The north–south transformations are equally important. The lot is graced with a serene due north mountain view and a complementary view south to the ocean. Movement along this axis connects a series of outside courtyards. One drives toward the mountain, along the eastern wall of the house to the parking court and then begins to move through a sequence of courts heading back toward the ocean view. Inside, the gallery and library emphasize the mountain to ocean axis. Outside, the terraced street links a series of courts.

The house itself is developed in close response to concerns of proportion and light. Its extruded shape was both economical and reminiscent of farmhouses in California and other warm coastal climates. Its tower and library reach for the ocean and mountain views animating the house along its street. Despite the tight footprint, the vertical movement of the house gives every room multiple views and breezes. The hearths focus life around the warm center of the house in winter. A sleeping porch, gallery, street, courts and

Project: Yudell/Beebe House
Size of Lot: 100 feet x 580 feet
Size of Project: 3,300 square feet
(main house), 970 square feet
(guest house)

Owner: Buzz Yudell and Tina Beebe
Architect: Buzz Yudell
Project Architect: Akai Ming-Kae Yang
Landscape: Tina Beebe
Color: Tina Beebe
Photography: Timothy Hursley
Model Shots: Craig Currie, Moore
Ruble Yudell Collection

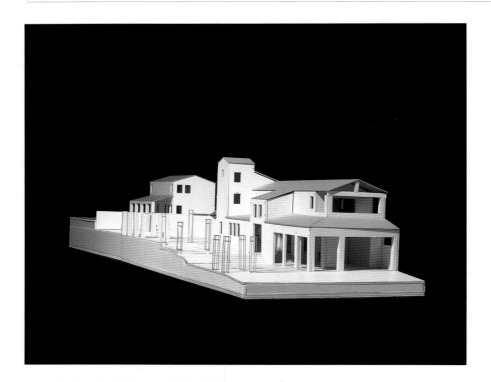

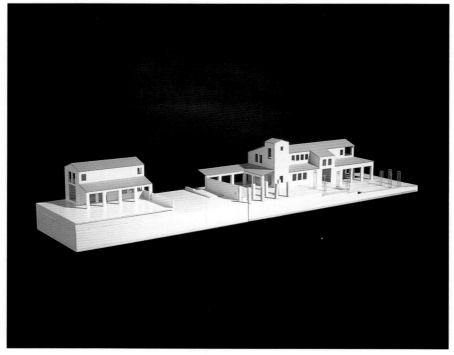

pergolas allow for connections to the benign climate and landscape much of the year.

The richness of experience derives from the overlay of the east–west transformation (formal rooms to native landscape) with the north–south, mountain to sea movement. The interplay of geometry, space, orientation and landscape creates a place that is at once serene and full of unfolding experiences.

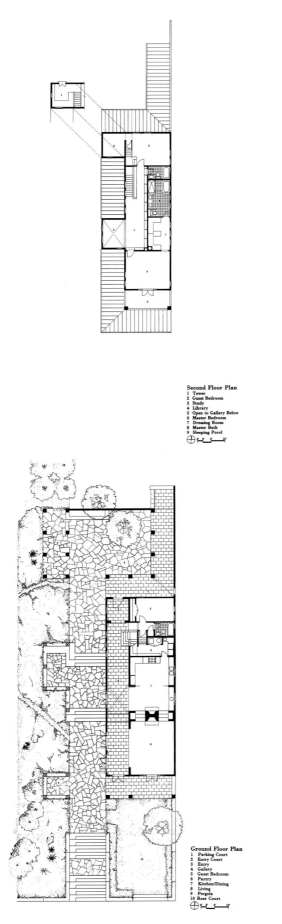

Second Floor Plan
1 Tower
2 Guest Bedroom
3 Study
4 Library
5 Open to Gallery Below
6 Master Bedroom
7 Dressing Room
8 Master Bath
9 Sleeping Porch

Ground Floor Plan
1 Parking Court
2 Entry Court
3 Entry
4 Gallery
5 Guest Bedroom
6 Pantry
7 Kitchen/Dining
8 Living
9 Pergola
10 Rose Court

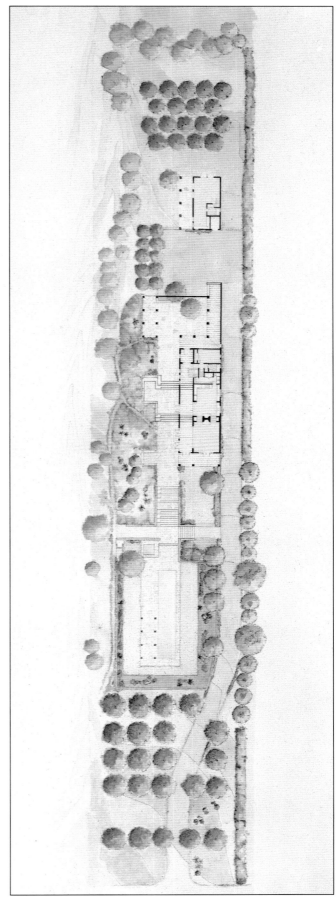

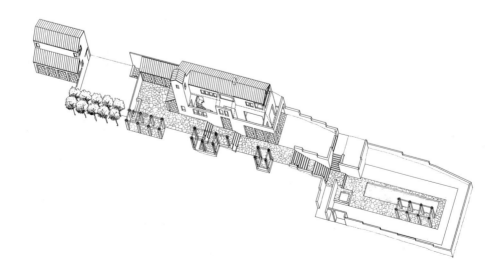

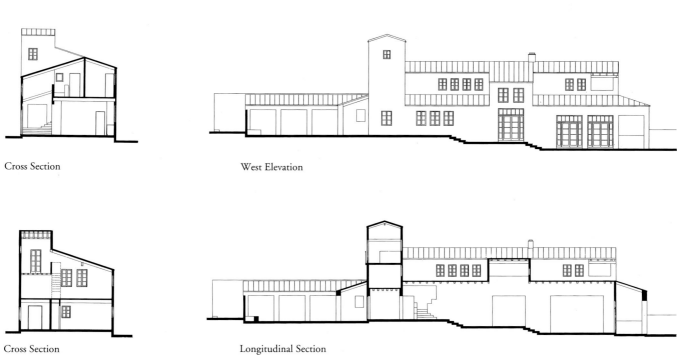

Cross Section

West Elevation

Cross Section

Longitudinal Section

South Elevation

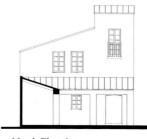

North Elevation

WALROD HOUSE
Berkeley, California

T his house is planned for the site of the family's original house which was lost to the Oakland/Berkeley fire of 1991. While the owners had lost their entire house, some of the remains of garden terraces and fountains survived. Seeking a sense of continuity and connection, these elements were preserved and integrated into the site plan and geometry of the new project. While the old house had been redolent of the Berkeley Hills, it had stood somewhat independent of the site. The new house is shaped to engage the terraced landscape. The clients wanted a house that would be quiet but rich with experiences. The house is modest and elemental.

From the street side a bridge over an entryway frames an exceptional view of the Golden Gate Bridge and a central tower anchors the house to its site. The gateway view is an offering to the public realm and the beginning of a sequence of carefully composed connections to landscape, both distant and close.

The garden or private side of the house is developed as a more plastic set of elements that link and terrace down the hillside. One can circulate equally through outside stairs and terraces or through a carefully choreographed internal sequence. Internally the calm of quietly proportioned rooms is contrasted by the complexity of the paths of movement.

The entire second floor of the main wing is seen as a redoubt for the parents. Bath, bedroom, and library are linked "en suite" by a generous porch which shades the south and west sun while framing views to the Bay.

This sequence is connected, by bridge, to a "tower" pavilion for one of the two sons. The second son's room is a "garden" pavilion at the other end of the sequence.

The relatively simple forms of the whole are composed to animate the site and heighten one's exploration of the land and views. As one inhabits this house there is always a sense of the special nature of the topography. The movement from garden to sky both orients us and allows for a diversity of experiences and emotions.

Project: Walrod House
Size of Lot: 17,090 square feet
Size of Project: 3,910 feet

Design Architect: Moore Ruble Yudell
Principal-in-Charge,
Pricipal Architect: Buzz Yudell
Principal Architect: John Ruble
Project Architect: Akai Ming-Kae Yang
Project Captain: Mark Peacor
Project Team: Tony Tran, Louis Bretana,
Craig Currie, Mark Grand
Color: Tina Beebe
Renderings: Tony Tran
Photography: Craig Currie, Moore Ruble
Yudell Collection

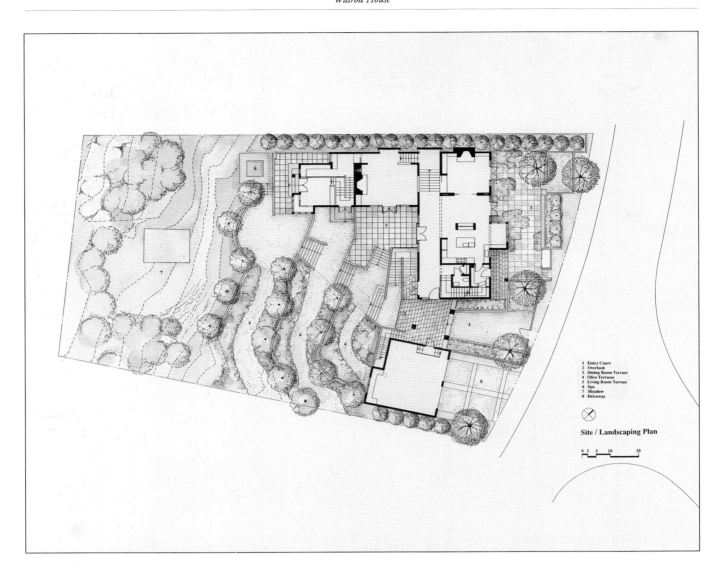

1 Entry Court
2 Overlook
3 Dining Room Terrace
4 Olive Terraces
5 Living Room Terrace
6 Spa
7 Meadow
8 Driveway

Site / Landscaping Plan

0 2 5   10   20

Second Floor Plan

1   Library
2   Sitting Room
3   Master Bedroom
4   Master Closet
5   Master Bathroom
6   Laundry Room
7   Hall
8   Study
9   Closet
10 Bathroom
11 Bedroom

0 2' 5'   10'   20'

Section

0 2' 5' 10'

Elevation

0 2' 5' 10' 20'

Section

0 2' 5' 10'

Elevation

0 2' 5' 10' 20'

VILLA SUPERBA
Venice, California

Much of the charm of beach towns like Venice and Santa Monica is found in their bungalow districts. Originally created for summer rental, the small wood cottages became a standard format for affordable housing in the 1920s and, '30s and suited our own needs in the hyper inflated housing market of the 1980s. Venice presents the most varied arrays — its walk streets, canal streets, circles and courts make it a lively thesaurus of patterns for contemporary housing. Superba Avenue itself, while not a walk-street, is centered in the walk-street district and shares its intimate scale. In expanding this Venice bungalow we hoped to set a good example for the neighborhood, in which charming small houses are too often scrapped for oversized stucco boxes.

In concept, the original house merges with a two-story addition, set politely back from the street and crowned by a rooftop sleeping porch. The original bungalow is rebuilt with the same lapped siding, while its wall-house companion is scaled up with painted plywood and horizontal battens. In the front, a remodelled and somewhat grander porch and glass roof-pyramid face the street behind a shallow garden of palms and jacarandas. At the back a walled courtyard, entered through glassy bays, is lushed up by banana trees, an outdoor fireplace and a small fountain.

The superimposing of the two "houses," and the interlocking of gardens, porches and window-bays, generate inside — outside ambiguities that are continued throughout: a hallway becomes a porch for the kitchen and stairway and the upstairs bedroom suite has its own house-like identity. In the familiar public to private sequence, the orderliness of the front rooms, framed by groups of columns, gives way upstairs to the idiosyncratic habitation of what seems more a freakishly high attic than a normal second story. In storybook fashion, rooms and windows stretch up and up, and an even taller ladder takes us through the roof, to distant views of the city, mountains and sea.

Project: Villa Superba
Size of Lot: 40 feet x 90 feet
Size of House: 1,650 square feet

Owner: John Ruble
Architect: John Ruble
Project Manager: Sylvia Deily,
Wendy Kohn
Photography: Timothy Hursley;
Model Shots by Craig Currie, Moore
Ruble Yudell Collection

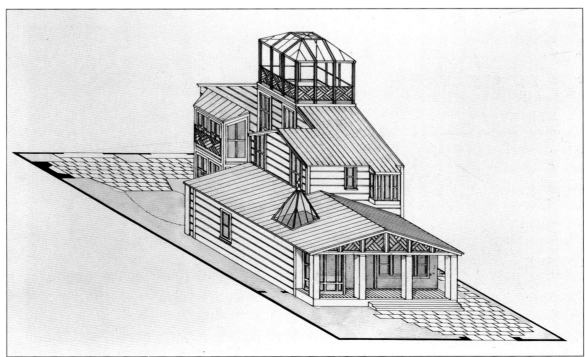

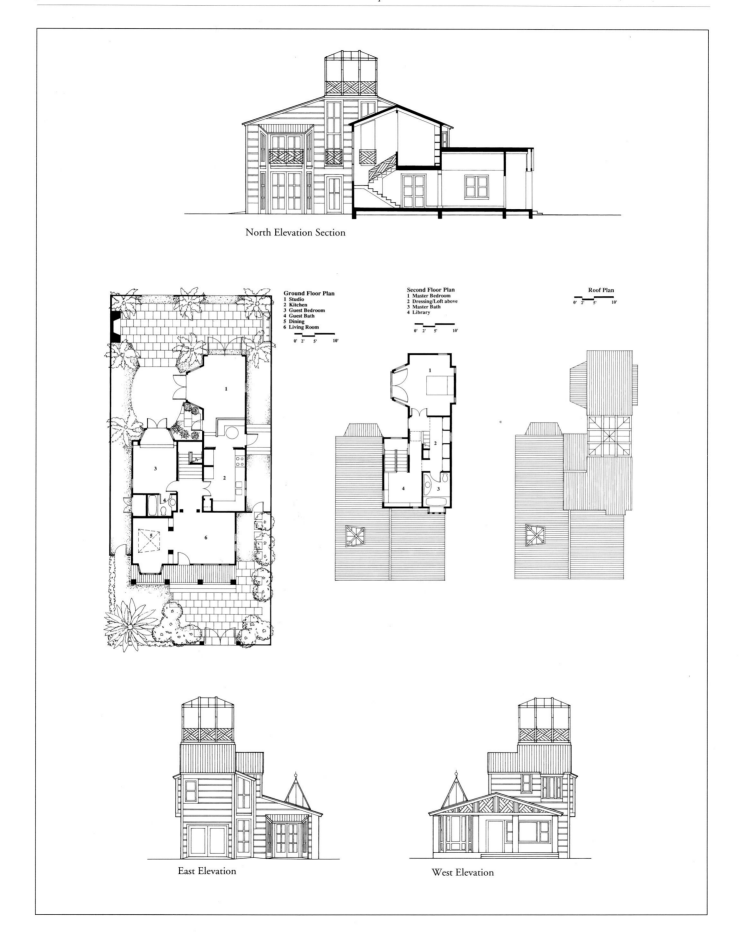

North Elevation Section

Ground Floor Plan
1 Studio
2 Kitchen
3 Guest Bedroom
4 Guest Bath
5 Dining
6 Living Room

0' 2' 5'   10'

Second Floor Plan
1 Master Bedroom
2 Dressing/Loft above
3 Master Bath
4 Library

0' 2' 5'   10'

Roof Plan

0' 2' 5'   10'

East Elevation

West Elevation

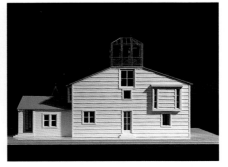

KWEE HOUSE
Singapore

This is a large house, almost on the equator, built for a young Singaporean in time to receive his bride, and later, some children. The library is for him the most important room; it lies at the heart of the house, linking in plan and section a larger courtyard and related formal rooms to a more intimate, informal courtyard and private rooms. The formal rooms, entry, living, dining and library, surround a long courtyard garden, shaded by a dramatic overhead trellis, filled with water and lush tropical flora. The guest room, playroom, and second-floor master suite, with its adjoining study overlooking the library, give onto a more intimate, formal garden court. The site has no views, no trees, and close neighbors, so the courtyards orient the house inward, for privacy, and give every room generous access to the outdoors. This access is all the more important because it is really only visual, due to the unremitting equatorial heat and humidity.

The simple gabled form of the house's exterior is quietly contextual; within, a rich choreography of layered light and color is revealed. Arcaded walls form a series of interconnected rectangles, their hues, varying subtly in value, ranging warmer towards the outside and cooler within. Their layering allows, simultaneously, the sense of discreet rooms and one of flowing, interconnected space. Along with the overhead trellises on the courtyards and openwork ceiling in the formal rooms, these layered walls carefully filter the strong equatorial light. The geometry of the walls creates a strong order for views and movement as well as an underlying proportional system that gives harmony to the rooms. The formal geometry and symmetry of architectural elements play against a more languid drift of water, tropical plants and human movement through the house.

Project: Kwee House
Size of Lot: 1,370 square meters
Size of House: 475 square meters

Owner: Liong Seen Kwee
Design Architect: Moore Ruble Yudell
Principal-in-Charge,
Principal Architect: Buzz Yudell
Principal Architect: Charles Moore
Principal Architect: John Ruble
Project Team: Tim Felchlin,
Liong Phing Kwee
Renderings: John Kyrk
Photography: Jaime Ardiles-Arce,
Courtesy of Architectural Digest

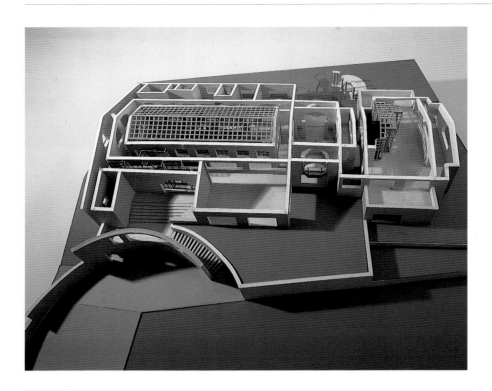

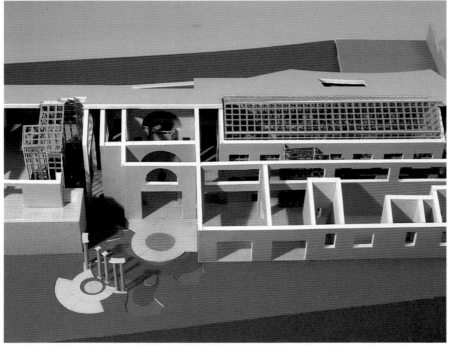

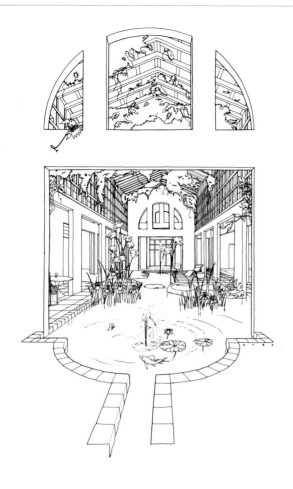

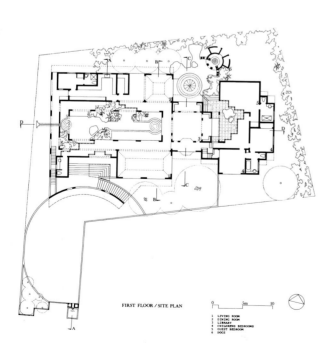

FIRST FLOOR / SITE PLAN

0   5m   10

1 LIVING ROOM
2 DINING ROOM
3 LIBRARY
4 CHILDRENS BEDROOMS
5 GUEST BEDROOM
6 DOGS

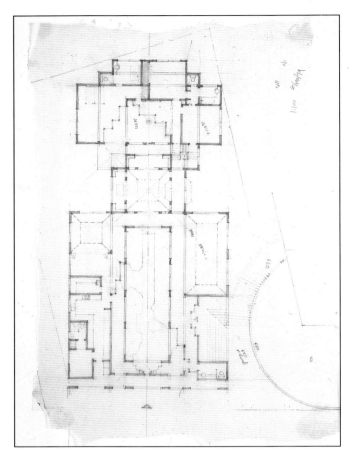

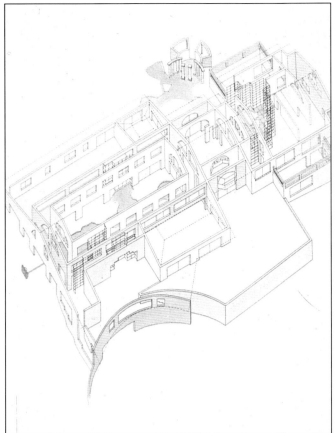

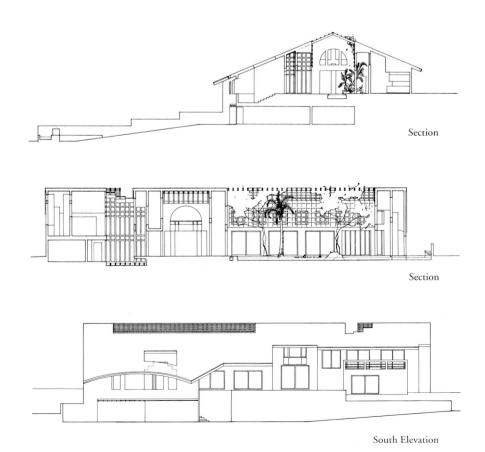

Section

Section

South Elevation

HOUSING

Housing Connections: Edges, Axes and Stories

John Ruble

While we have seen that each single house gives us the chance to create a whole world, we have also learned that housing projects are fragments — partial worlds which are dependent on their context for meaning. Features and qualities of the site, and its urban setting, become even more important as the sequence of places and dwellings within the project draws on connections to a surrounding town and landscape.

These connections can take the form of carefully fit edges: In Karow Nord and Potatisåkern the scale and building format both reflect and complement neighboring development, creating a gentle boundary. At Playa Vista a nearly seamless edge is created toward each of four radically different neighboring features: a restored wetland toward the sea, an expanded marina with luxury housing toward Marina del Rey, a linear park toward the bluffs to the south, and commercial development alongside existing light industry to the east. At Tegel Harbor, the village side of the project presents a series of views and walks to the harbor side, framed by pairs of urban villas.

Tegel suggests a second strategy: drawing linear movement and views into the site, creating connections by invitation and continuity. Potatisåkern uses a series of such axial links to surrounding streets, and adds diagonals, the curved line of the "snake" buildings which continue a nearby meandering lane and a long axial vista from the front of a German church, from across one corner of the site all the way to Golden Sound at the far end. At Karow Nord, an existing network of small north–south streets is directly woven into the project, as broad stripes of open land roll across from east to west — a woof and warp of bi-axial movement linking the new housing to village and field.

In apparent exception to these tendencies, Kobe Nishiokamoto goes to considerable lengths to frame its own world. Its connection to the city is as formal as a grand hotel, with a strongly walled perimeter. Inside, formally composed towers and courtyard buildings embrace a series of gardens. The gardens themselves represent Japan's island ethos — "from the mountains to the sea" — and connect the inhabitants to a mythic place of origin, in a kind of story line. This use of story, derived from aspects of place, in turn reflects on the inhabitants and their "moment" in a long history of the use of the land. Others came before, and presumably others will come after, and the hope is that this overlay of human settlements will retain some measure of meaning, gathering up each story, rather than discarding them. A good example is Tegel Harbor, where the old harbor itself becomes a central figure, expanded into the site to become even more significant in the urban transformation, with its recreation island-boat oriented towards the lakes of the Havel beyond. Given the many impacts of new development, and its inevitable effect on the quality of life of any neighboring settlement, we find this conservation of memory and meaning to be essential to community building.

However successfully we are guided by these concerns, the most important value for housing is its *wohnqualität* — its quality as home. Perhaps it is our recent experience in Europe and Japan, where the complex web of standards and rules place extreme limits on apartment planning, which has taught us the value of fully using the site and its adjacencies to create a living environment. Each aspect of site planning — views, gardens, the placement of play and recreation, the sequence of arrival — adds a vital dimension to high density living and makes for success or failure in the creation of community place.

Of at least equal importance to architecture in this effort is the treatment of the landscape itself: in all the projects, we have been fortunate to have strong and imaginative allies in landscape design.

Embedded in this interpretive landscape are the hundreds or thousands of apartments which must mean home to each inhabitant. In Europe, even the smallest apartment usually features two places where we can feel we are at the center of our world, and it seems above all critical that they are well provided for. One is a place for a dining table with a simple lamp hanging over it (European condominiums and apartments rarely feature that mythic American home-center, the fireplace). This is captured in Van Gogh's "The Potato Eaters": the kind of gathering place and act of habitation that virtually defines us as human beings. The second "center" is ironically at the edge of the plan: a balcony or loggia. The balcony establishes contact with the world beyond, is always filled with light, and may even contain dried-up pots of plants which remind us in winter that warmer months do exist, and will soon return. In summer, the small space which subsidy boards allocate to living rooms magically expands to include the balcony and some part of the gardens outside. We look for ways to give identity to this vital spot, that it may be recognized from the outside as you approach, giving each home its unique place in the street or courtyard.

As one of our German clients noted, nothing is more challenging for the architect than designing good housing — he then gave us two weeks to design over 100 units. Indeed, however well-intentioned we are, the architect/developer/public agency nexus itself adds a good deal to the difficulties. As the actual inhabitants are only represented in the abstract, by public housing standards and developer marketing trends, we draw increasingly on our experiences and attitudes formed in collaboration with homeowners, and ask ourselves — would you want to live there?—as an ultimate test.

Three recent projects — Karow Nord and Kirchsteigfeld in Germany, and Playa Vista in California — are of the scale of town planning. While these projects still have all the issues of connection to their surroundings, they are large enough to involve their own internal hierarchies — centers and subcenters within an urban network. Notions of "town" and "townscape," with hints of "garden suburb" in the pre-war sense, have replaced the repetitive architectural composition of "the projects" in each of these places.

The basic element is the garden block, a village-sized city block with a careful proportion of building-to-open space and, in the German model, a detailed hierarchy of private and semi-private landscape at the block interior. Outside, the scale and proportion of a range of boulevards, avenues and alleys are made-to-order, challenging the bureaucratic inheritance of traffic planning and other public agency assumptions, in the campaign for livable streets. Centers, in the form of gardens, public facilities, schools, and supporting commercial activity, are carefully composed within the urban network, giving special identity to adjacent housing. The housing itself is presented in a broad array of building types, from duplex houses to perimeter blocks of flats, each providing its best, most characteristic pattern of open space.

Overlaying these patterns, cutting across the whole fabric, or bending, twisting, and shearing the urban network, are the existing, sometimes latent features of the site. Remnants and textures of historic use, whether urban or agricultural, are still to be discovered, and even celebrated, giving each project a unique physical connection with its land and culture.

Top: General View of Tegel Harbor
Berlin, Germany
Photograph by Richard Bryant

Bottom: Nishiokamoto Housing Entrance
Kobe, Japan
Photograph by Timothy Hursley

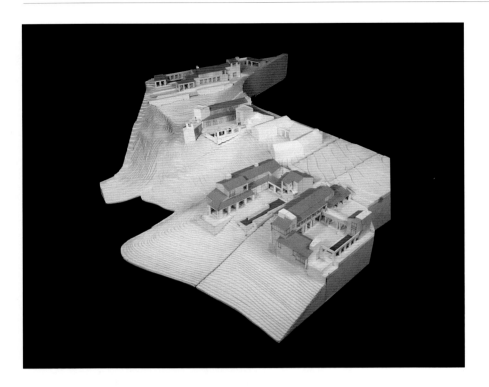

MALIBU HOUSES
Malibu, California

Several acres along a coastal bluff near Point Dume are the site for ten large single-family houses. Our client asked us to create a master plan and design four of the houses in a way that would give each house a distinctive character and allow them to work together as a unified composition. The houses needed to respond to a careful balance between the sense of individuality and the developer's need to have certain repetitive elements for cost savings. Seeing them as a "family" of houses created a conceptual structure for this synthesis.

The land rises steeply from the Pacific Coast Highway to a series of small ridges and canyons. Composed as a group, the houses are nestled along the ridges to take advantage of the commanding views but to offer each one privacy from its neighbors. Garages are grouped around shared auto courts. Each house is articulated to respond to its particular site and orientation in distinctive ways.

The houses are made of simple forms, articulated by sloping tile roofs, parapets, arcades, pergolas and bay windows. Each house, with its garage and pool house, is organized around an outdoor courtyard. The courtyard offers protection from the wind to the pool and outdoor living areas and frames the view beyond. French doors and windows onto the courtyard work to break the distinctions between indoors and out. The landscape is predominantly composed of restored native species along all the slopes and valley areas. Courtyards are typically hard surfaces integrated with small areas of cultivated landscape.

A palette of shared materials and colors links to the landscape and unifies the houses. Houses by other architects would be related by color, material and landscape while expressing their individual characters. We would hope for a hilltop village which connects to the landscape and expresses the dialogue among the houses.

Project: Malibu Houses
Size of Lots: Lot I (32,400 square feet);
Lot II (32,790 square feet);
Lot IV (46,500 square feet);
Lot V (45,100 square feet)
Size of Projects: House I (5,400 square feet); House II (4,900 square feet); House IV (4,900 square feet); House V (4,700 square feet)

Design Architect: Moore Ruble Yudell
Principal Architect: Charles Moore
Principal Architect: John Ruble
Principal Architect: Buzz Yudell
Project Architect: Daniel Garness
Team Captain: Akai Ming-Kae Yang
Project Team: Mario Violich, Cynthia Phakos, Tony Anella, Anthony Tam, Richard Destin
Renderings: Daniel Garness, Tony Tran
Photography: Craig Currie, Moore Ruble Yudell Collection

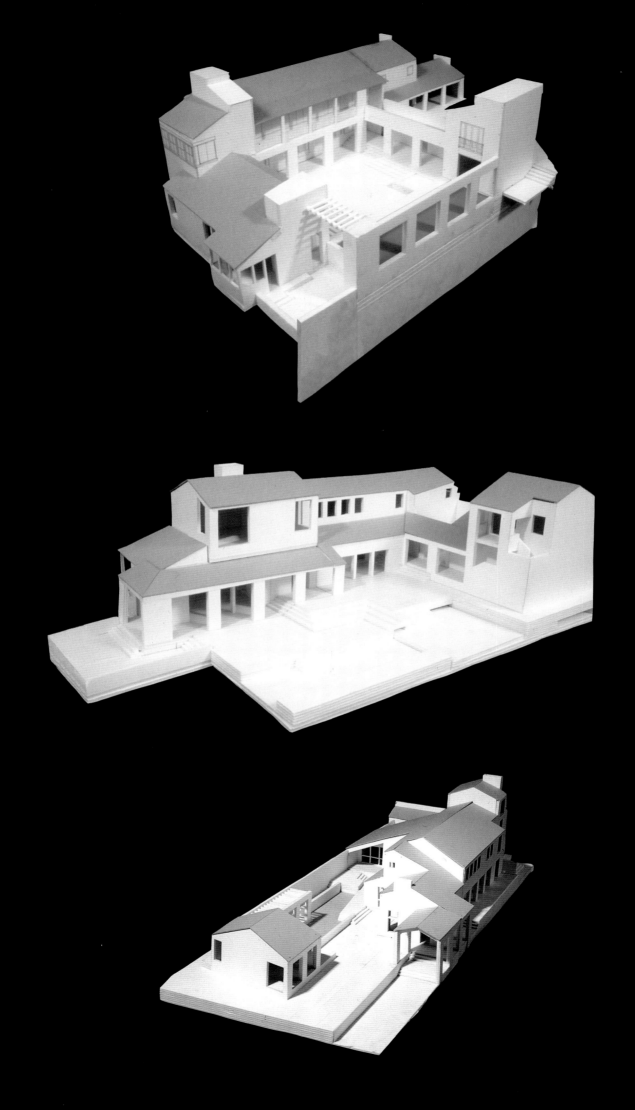

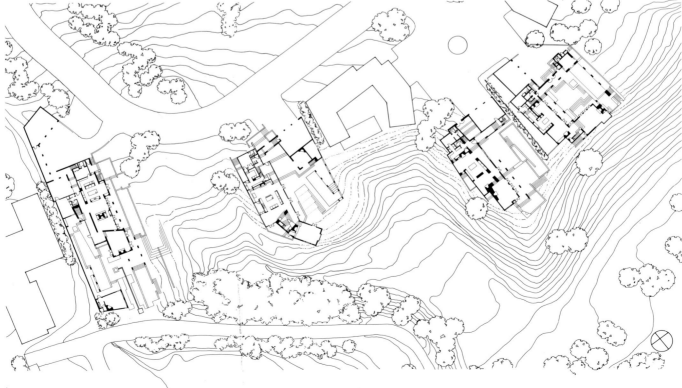

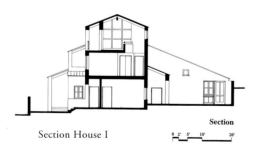

Section House I

Elevation House I

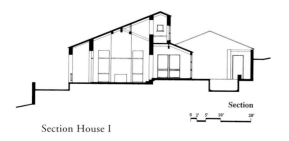

Section House I

Elevation House I I

PLAYA VISTA MASTER PLAN
Los Angeles, California

Playa Vista is a major new urban development encompassing nearly 900 acres of largely undeveloped land at the heart of Los Angeles' Westside. In 1989 we were asked to participate in a team of planners and architects to create a master plan for Playa Vista to include 11,750 units of housing, five million square feet of office space, 720,000 square feet of retail space, 2,400 hotel rooms and a 40-acre marina. Our challenge was to address social and environmental concerns within the economic constraints of our clients to create an appropriate urban model for new development in Los Angeles.

Our first challenge was the notion of community: understanding what contributes to the sense of community in a place, and how traditional techniques and patterns of development might inform approaches to more contemporary issues, from public transportation to waste treatment and recycling. We began by analyzing precedents and traditional concepts of urban development to invest in Playa Vista the vitality and appeal of our favorite cities. Our strategy came to include a combination of traditional techniques, including mixed-use, mid-density, mid-rise planning, and the re-establishment of the importance of civic and cultural amenities as essential elements of the community.

Over 270 acres of existing wetlands on the site were to be preserved. On the remaining land, an ordered system of blocks and streets — interspersed with parks, open areas and greenbelts linked by pedestrian paths — weaves the new community into the fabric of the surrounding city. Retail, civic and office uses were distributed among residential areas so that each unit of housing is within walking distance of transit, stores, schools, open space or places to work. A diversity of housing types, drawn from successful Southern California precedents, offers a range of choices for housing and includes 25% affordable units.

Project: Playa Vista Master Plan
Size of Lot: 947 acres
Size of Project: 11,000 units of housing, office, hotel, retail, civic and cultural buildings; a 40-acre marina and 270 acres of restored wetlands.

Owner/Client: Maguire Thomas Partners
Design Architect: Moore Ruble Yudell
Principal-in-Charge,
Principal Architect: Buzz Yudell
Principal Architect: Charles Moore
Principal Architect: John Ruble
Project Team: Curtis Woodhouse, Doug Jamieson, Mary Beth Elliott, Mark Peacor, John Johnson, Mario Violich, Linda Brettler, Craig Currie, John Taft
Associated Planning Team Members: Hanna/Olin Ltd., Legorretta Arquitectos, Moule Polyzoides, Duany Plater-Zyberk
Renderings: Curtis Woodhouse, Doug Jamieson, Tony Tran
Photography: Moore Ruble Yudell Collection

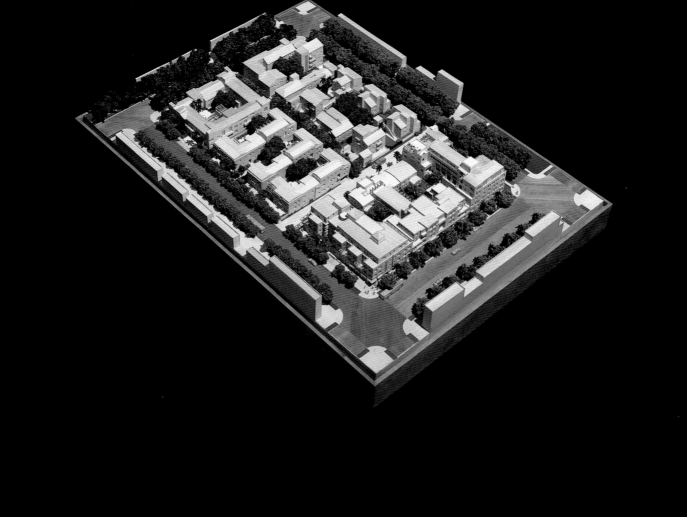

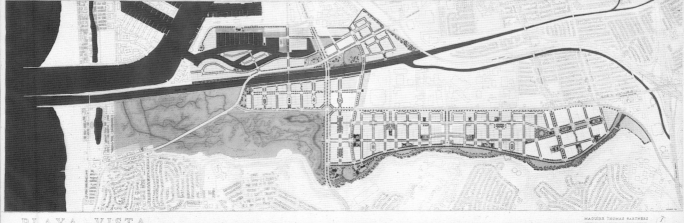

PLAYA VISTA

MAGUIRE THOMAS PARTNERS

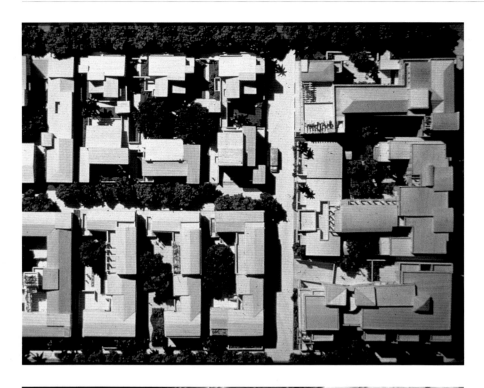

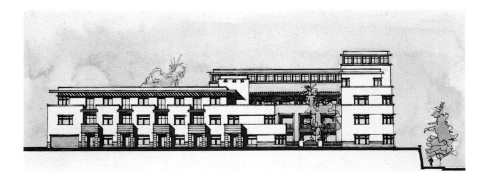

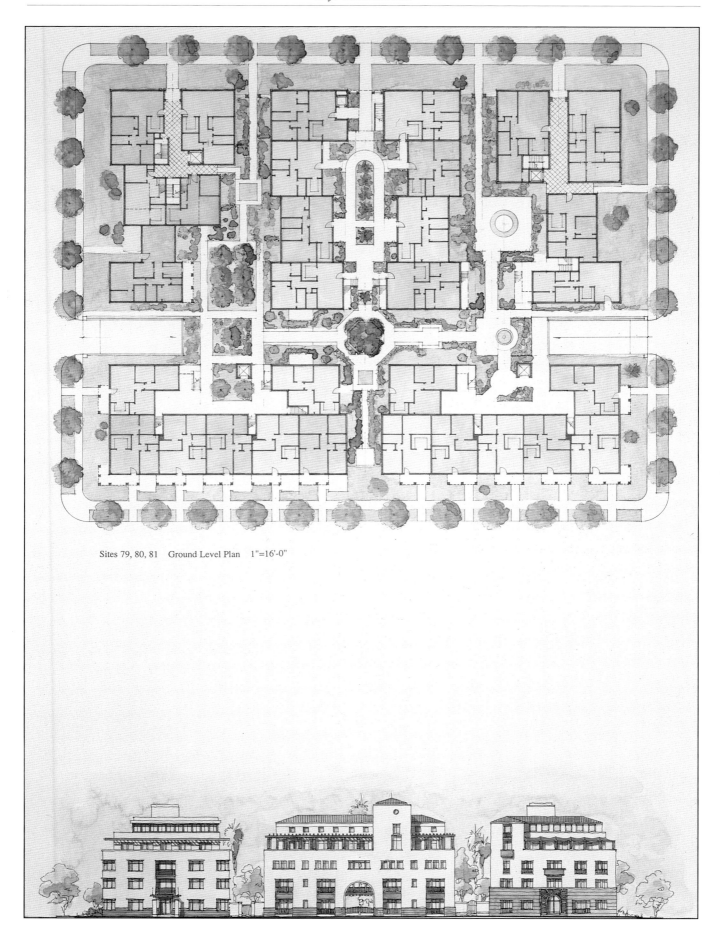

Sites 79, 80, 81   Ground Level Plan   1"=16'-0"

KOBE NISHIOKAMOTO HOUSING
Kobe, Japan

Southeast of Osaka, on Japan's inland sea, lies Kobe. Since the establishment of the city as a port in 1868, Kobe has been host to periods of intense foreign settlement, and exposure to many ideas and cultures. Our client sought a design for 300 condominiums that would reflect western influence, provide a landmark that would appeal to their clients, and offer a resort-like atmosphere.

We began by trying to make the closest possible connection between the buildings and the landscape. The site, once a rolling hillside with a natural spring, had been radically graded into flat pads for barracks-like post-war housing. Our master plan involved the restoration of the topography and the configuration of perimeter buildings around a sequence of gardens. The plan is based on the concept of a formal axis between the city and the mountains crossing an informal axis of gardens running with the topography of the land and reflecting the site's position between the mountains and the sea.

The buildings step from three to eight floors, with a pair of 11-story towers framing the formal axis and centering the project at the crossing of the axes. Composed of stone, plaster and concrete, the buildings rise to glazed winter gardens where they meet pitched roofs and dormers.

The gardens are a narrative to be experienced either individually, or as a continuous journey. A stream rises from a hidden source within the mountain garden, winds through the meadow garden — a pastoral interlude — is interrupted by the waterfall crossing of the formal axis, and comes to rest in the ocean garden. The formal entry ellipse, enlivened by topiary, leads through a dignified allée of magnolia trees, stops at an overlook of the waterfall crossing, and ends in a quiet white garden — the completion of the formal axis.

In this project, we welcomed the challenge of layering public garden areas with more private gardens, and at the same time enhancing the individual character of the private residences.

Project: Kobe Nishiokamoto Housing
Size of Lot: 9 acres
Size of Project: 315 units of condominiums

Owners: Mitsui Real Estate Development
Co., Ltd.; Haseko Corporation; Kawasaki
Heavy Industries Ltd.; Mitsui & Co. Ltd.
Design Architect: Moore Ruble Yudell
Principal-in-Charge,
Principal Architect: Buzz Yudell
Principal Architect: Charles Moore
Principal Architect: John Ruble
Project Architect: James Mary O'Connor
Mary Beth Elliott, James B. Morton
Project Liaison: Shuji Kurokawa
Project Team: Go Miyashiro, Wing-hon
Ng, Michihiro Ota, John Taft, Steve
Gardner, George Venini, Ying-Chao Kuo
Landscape Team-Project Manager: Daniel
Garness; Landscape Design Consultant:
Tina Beebe, Mario Violich, Akai Ming-Kae
Yang; Landscape Production Consultant:
Tetsuo Hanawa; Toyo Landscape
Construction Co. Ltd.; Junji Yoshikawa;
Production Architect: Mitsui Construction
Co. Ltd –Tamio Sanpei, Ryouichi Misawa,
Satoshi Matsubara, Takao Ito, Mitsuru
Nishikawa, Mitsuhiro Sugiyama
Color: Tina Beebe
Renderings: James Mary O'Connor,
Curtis Woodhouse
Model Shots: Craig Currie
Photography: Timothy Hursley

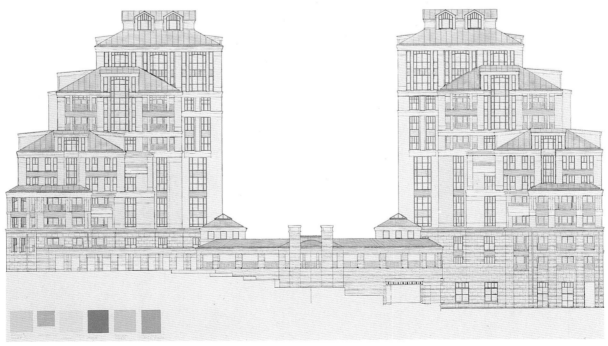

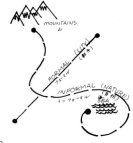

Concepts

Landmarks

Types of Spaces

Landscape

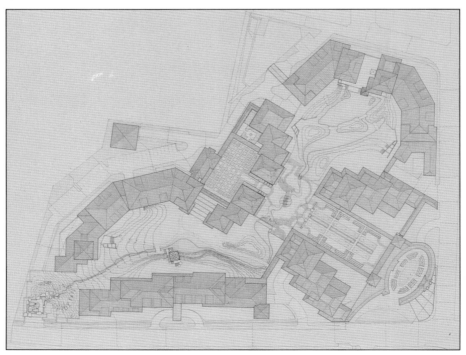

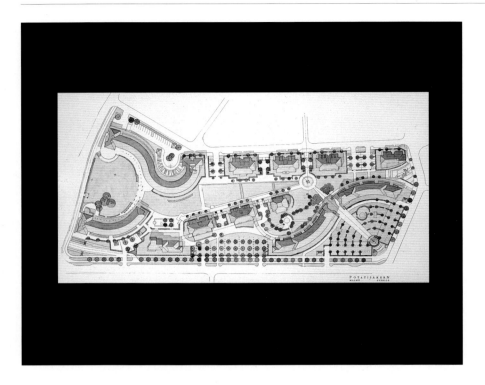

POTATISÅKERN HOUSING

Malmo, Sweden

Along the Öresund (Golden Sound), which separates Sweden from Denmark, the City of Malmö owns a large tract of undeveloped land, which was until recently a potato field, in the midst of an established suburban neighborhood. Various proposals for the land, dating from the 1930s, have been rejected by the City as inappropriate for this important site. When we were asked to prepare a master plan for this land our primary goal was to continue established patterns of development by creating an urban design sensitive to various surrounding conditions, one which would link the waterfront to the adjacent community and the city beyond.

As the site plan took shape, its focus became two large urban gestures. At the waterfront a large crescent embraces the water and the view. Behind this crescent a broad, gently sloping expanse of lawn bounded by an allée of trees and 16-unit "villas" runs the length of the property. This lawn creates an axis linking the waterfront to an existing church and the neighborhoods beyond, and ties together a sequence of varied open spaces throughout the site.

The buildings on the site are of two basic types: long sinuous curves that reflect the curving streetscape of the nearby Friluftsstad, and 16-unit "villas" that respond to the suburban villas in flanking residential districts. A discrete set of traditional architectural elements — balconies, chimneys, winter gardens, pitched roofs, "punched openings" and arcades — unifies the buildings. Landscaping takes advantage of the mature trees around the site, and varies, to give each open area individuality as an outdoor room.

Local materials such as metal roofs and sack-rubbed brick walls reinforce the consistency of the new buildings with their context. The sinuous curves of the "snake" are rendered in subdued but warm tones, to serve as a backdrop for the villas, whose colors are derived from the Swedish tradition of brightness, appropriate for Malmö's even light.

Project: Potatisåkern Housing
Size: of Lot: 10 acres
Size of Project: 327 units of 29,709,
square meters or 316,000 square feet

Owner: MKB; Skanska
Design Architect: Moore Ruble Yudell
Principal-in-Charge,
Principal Architect: John Ruble
Principal Architect: Charles Moore
Principal Architect: Buzz Yudell
Project Architect: Cecily Young
Project Architect, Concept Phase: Renzo Zecchetto
Project Team: Ying-Chao Kuo, Chris Duncan, Tea Sapo, Yeon Keun Jeong, Mary Beth Elliott, Steven Gardner, John Taft, Tony Tran, James Mary O'Connor, Wing-Hon Ng, Craig Currie, Mark Grand
Color: Tina Beebe
Renderings: George Nakatani
Executive Architect: Hultin & Lundquist Arkitekter AB, (Kurt Hultin, Dennis Johnsson) in joint venture with FFNS Arkitekter I Skåne AB, Malmö (Bertil Öhrström)
Photography: Lars Cardell, Moore Ruble Yudell Collection

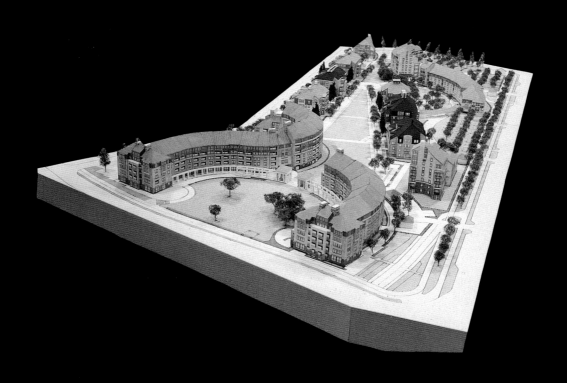
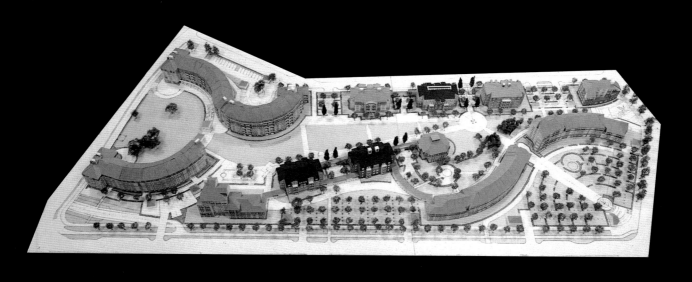

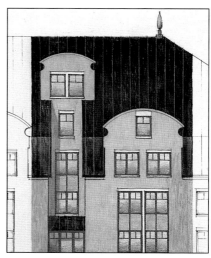

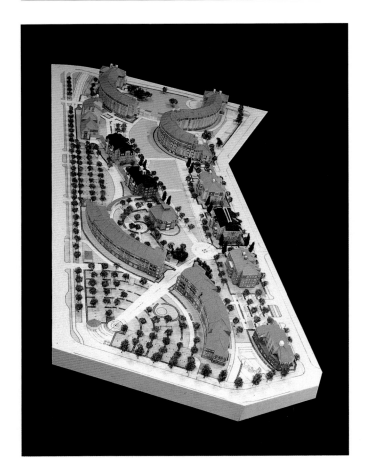

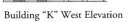

Building "K" West Elevation   Building "U" West Elevation

Building "P" North Elevation

Building "G" North Elevation

Building "F" North Elevation

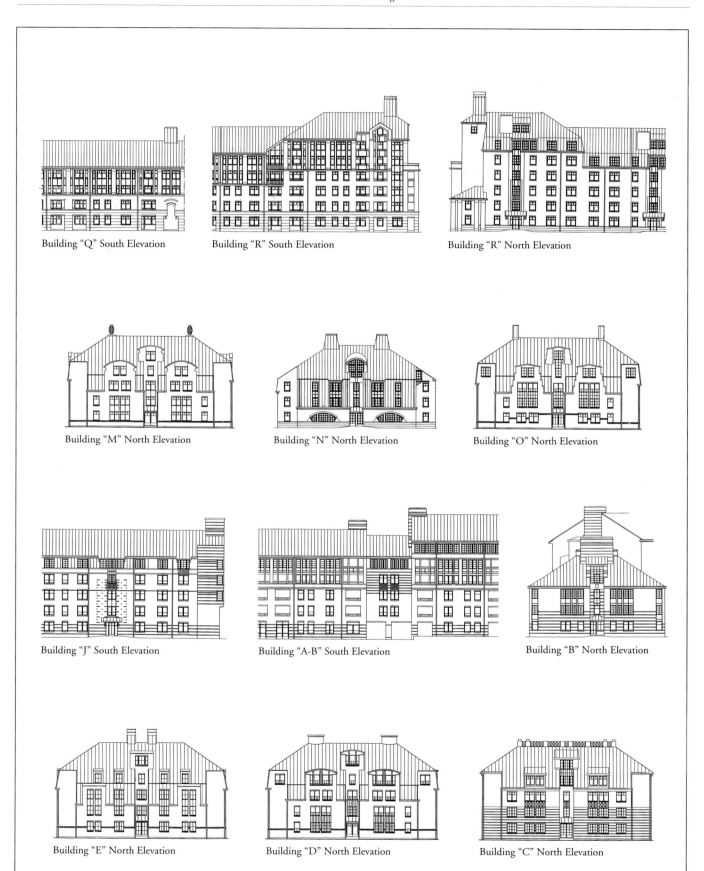

Building "Q" South Elevation   Building "R" South Elevation   Building "R" North Elevation

Building "M" North Elevation   Building "N" North Elevation   Building "O" North Elevation

Building "J" South Elevation   Building "A-B" South Elevation   Building "B" North Elevation

Building "E" North Elevation   Building "D" North Elevation   Building "C" North Elevation

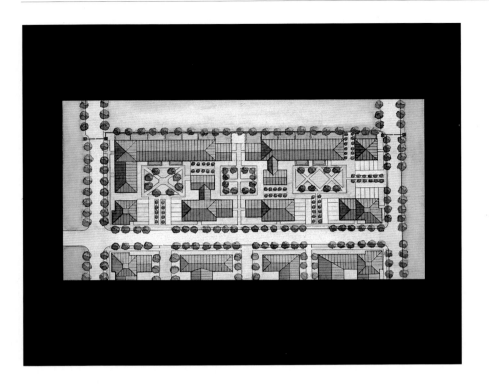

KONSTANCIN HOUSING

Konstancin, Poland

This project creates a new residential development that responds to the unique historical and environmental qualities of Konstancin, a community located near Warsaw and known for the quality of its climate and recreational areas. The project follows the spirit of the area's tradition of clean air, forests and health spas. Our goal is to create a community that begins with the best qualities of local precedents and simultaneously incorporates the advantages of contemporary planning and construction.

The project is organized in close relationship to the geometry and patterns of Konstancin's historic fabric. View corridors and landscaped passages visually extend the adjacent streets of Konstancin toward the new residential areas. The plan begins with its character as a pedestrian-oriented village-like neighborhood, with heavily landscaped streets encouraging pedestrian passage and interaction. Neighborhood parks allow for a high ratio of recreational and landscape spaces to built areas, while maintaining a diverse range of spaces. A formal axis makes a strong north–south connection as the central landscaped boulevard of the project, while to the east and west more informally organized neighborhoods are focused around their individual neighborhood parks. The whole pattern is woven together by the fabric of the streets to form one integral neighborhood village.

Hierarchies of public-to-private spaces transition from larger parks to mid-block pedestrian paths and finally to small private or semi-private gardens.

Similarly, the housing units themselves are carefully scaled and varied. Along the major boulevard, houses are more formally organized. Closer to the lake they become more articulated and allow for view corridors.

Hierarchies in open spaces, streets, passages, and landscaping as well as the balance of harmony and diversity within the architectural expression contribute to a neighborhood village which can be a sensitive neighbor in the wider context of Konstancin and Warsaw.

Project: Konstancin Housing
Size of Lot: 62 acres
Size of Project: 260 units

Client: Dumas West & Co.
Director: Brian Garrison
Design Architect: Moore Ruble Yudell
Principal-in-Charge,
Principal Architect: Buzz Yudell
Principal Architect: Charles Moore
Principal Architect: John Ruble
Project Architect: James Mary O'Connor
Project Team: Cecily Young, George Venini, Tony Tran, Mark Peacor, Wing-Hon Ng, Steve Gardner
Renderings: James Mary O'Connor, Tony Tran

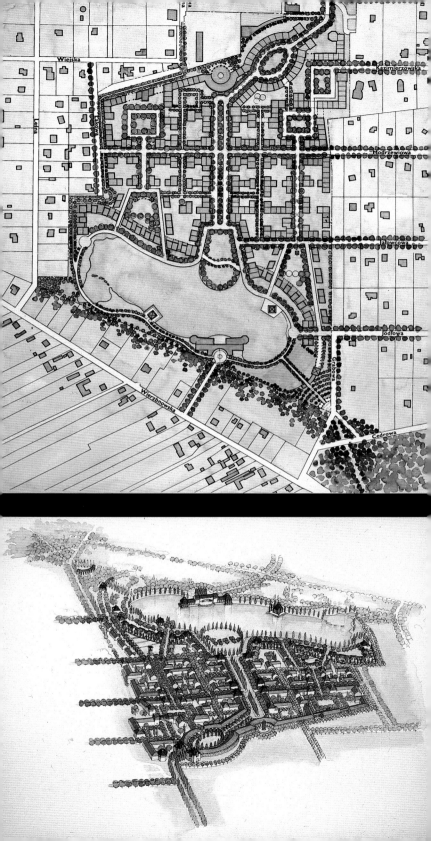

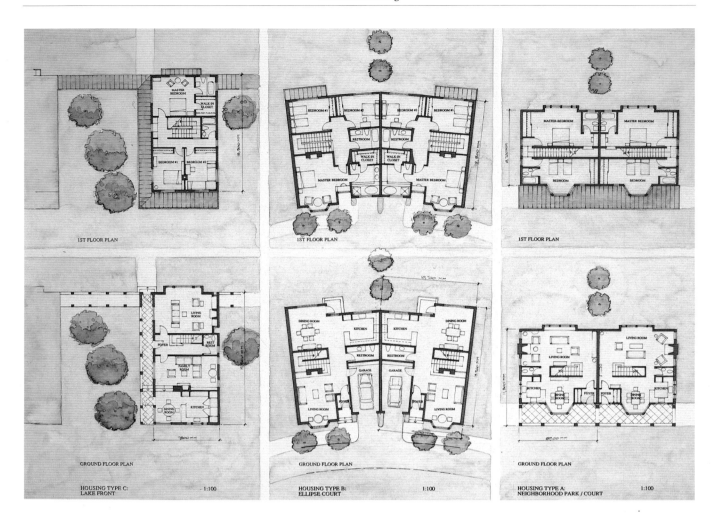

1ST FLOOR PLAN

1ST FLOOR PLAN

1ST FLOOR PLAN

GROUND FLOOR PLAN

GROUND FLOOR PLAN

GROUND FLOOR PLAN

HOUSING TYPE C:
LAKE FRONT   1:100

HOUSING TYPE B:
ELLIPSE COURT   1:100

HOUSING TYPE A:
NEIGHBORHOOD PARK / COURT   1:100

TEGEL HARBOR MASTER PLAN

Berlin, Germany

Tegel Harbor connects a delightful village with a chain of lakes and canals, as well as forested open space, which provide Berliners with weekend outings, seemingly far from the city center. The program of this international competition, which we won in 1980, called for residential, cultural and sports recreation uses.

This 170-unit housing complex forms the first part of the multi-use master plan. An additional 150 units within our master plan were designed by other architects as a second phase of construction.

The housing area makes a rich and varied set of connections between Tegel Village and a small harbor, whose expansion and conversion to recreational use is also part of the master plan. Bounded on one side by Seventh Street, the housing begins with a series of bright villas, embraced by a second layer of gently undulating row houses. Within the row house sequence, our project establishes a courtyard with four "houses" and four gates. The axis of this court proceeds directly through two of these gates to the landscaped commons beyond, ending with a view of the harbor. This visual axis to the water is seconded by a meandering path lined with tall poplars. In the great commons, the houses step up from five stories to eight, plus a high zinc-covered roof. The roof is itself a lively village of dormer windows and loggias, set upon a more ordered base of stucco walls with precast pilasters and moldings.

The social housing units are tiny, by code, yet are relieved by generous loggias. Typical units allow views to both the commons — to the south — and the harbor — generally north — from their combined living/dining rooms.

The design seeks to achieve an extraordinary degree of variety within a pre-cast concrete construction system, making this high-density social "townhousing" at once urbane and playful. The chance for both individual and collective identity in social housing has made this amongst the most sought–after housing in Berlin.

Project: Tegel Harbor Master Plan
Size of Lot: 26 acres
Size of Project: 170 units, 200,000 square feet

Owner: Beta Siebente
Design Architect: Moore Ruble Yudell
Principal-in-Charge,
Principal Architect: John Ruble
Principal Architect: Charles Moore
Principal Architect: Buzz Yudell
Project Architect: Thomas Nagel
Project Team: Leon Glodt, Regina Pizzinini, Peter Zingg, Eileen Liebman, Mel Lawrence
Associated Architect: Händel, Wolf und Zell
Landscape: Müller Knippschild Wehberg
Lighting: Richard C. Peters
Color: Tina Beebe
Renderings: William Hersey
Photography: Timothy Hursley, except page 160,162 by Richard Bryant; and page 161 by John Ruble, Moore Ruble Yudell Collection
Model Shots: Craig Currie, Moore Ruble Yudell Collection

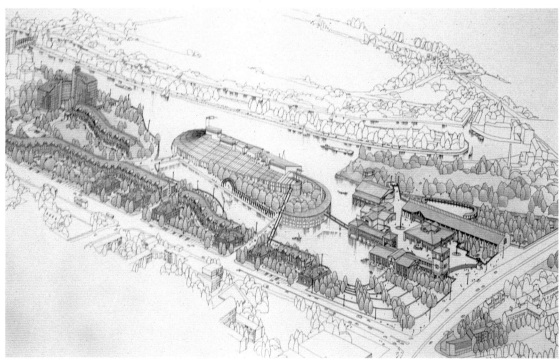

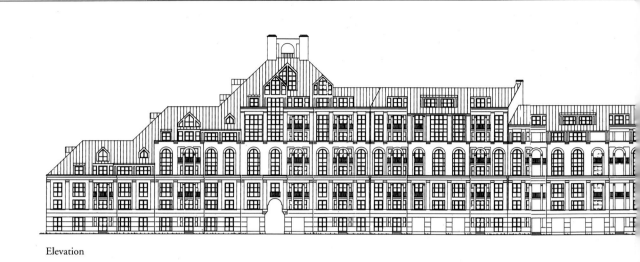

Elevation

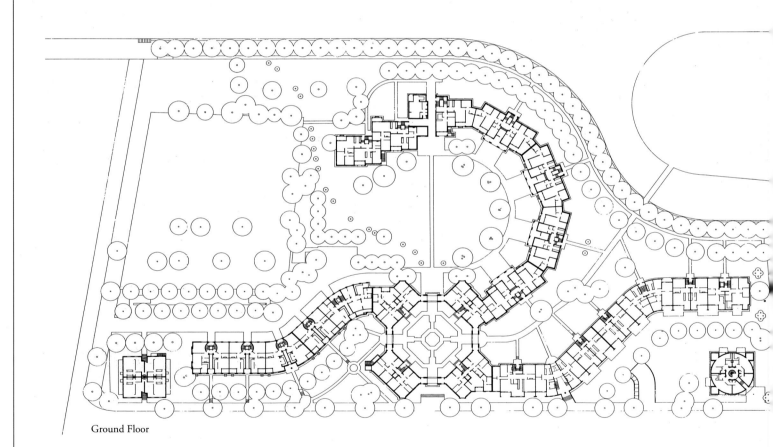

Ground Floor

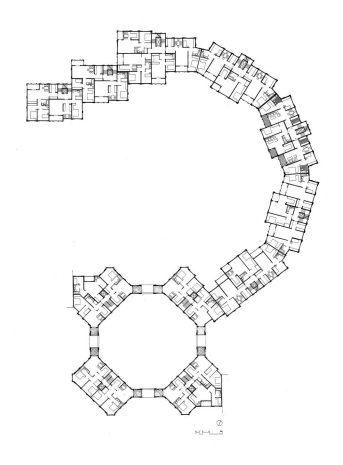

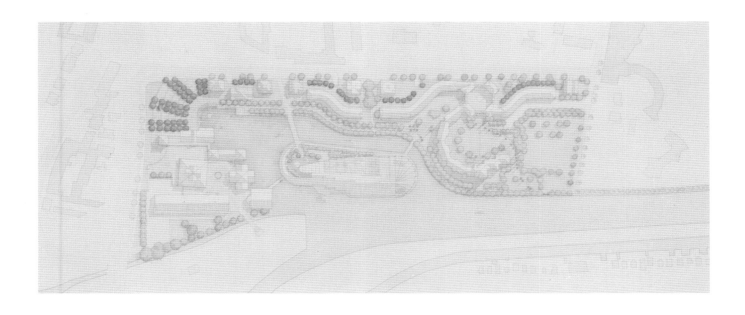

TEGEL VILLA
Berlin, Germany

This multi-unit building is one of six, all designed by various architects to respond to our master plan and design guidelines for the Tegel site. They all share the formal notion of a freestanding urban "villa." Each one is influenced by its particular location within the plan, and they all play colorfully as "signature" works against the more restrained baseline of the row houses.

Ours is adjacent to the entry plaza, and so it must make a kind of preamble to the rest of the project — which it does in two ways. First, it includes a small courtyard entered through a gate, hinting at grander courts and gardens to come. Secondly, it is highly articulated, using formal devices which are recollected when they are revealed later in much larger buildings down the harbor.

In program our villa differs from the others: it is used for professional and doctors' offices rather than apartments.

The villa typology was of special interest for the way in which they can have individual identity and even diversity of uses, while still relating to one another as an "urban set." Toward this end we wrote guidelines that established footprints and massing envelopes but allowed for expression as diverse as the other architects who were invited to design villas: Hejduk, Portoghesi, Tigerman, Stern and Grumbach.

Project: Tegel Villa
Size of Lot: Part of Tegel Housing

Owner: Beta Siebente
Design Architect: Moore Ruble Yudell
Principal-in-Charge,
Principal Architect: John Ruble
Principal Architect: Charles Moore
Principal Architect: Buzz Yudell
Project Architect: Thomas Nagel
Project Team: Leon Glodt, Regina Pizzinini
Associated Architect: Händel, Wolf und Zell
Landscape: Müller Knippschild Wehberg
Color: Tina Beebe
Photography: Timothy Hursley; except page 166 bottom left, by Buzz Yudell, Moore Ruble Yudell Collection

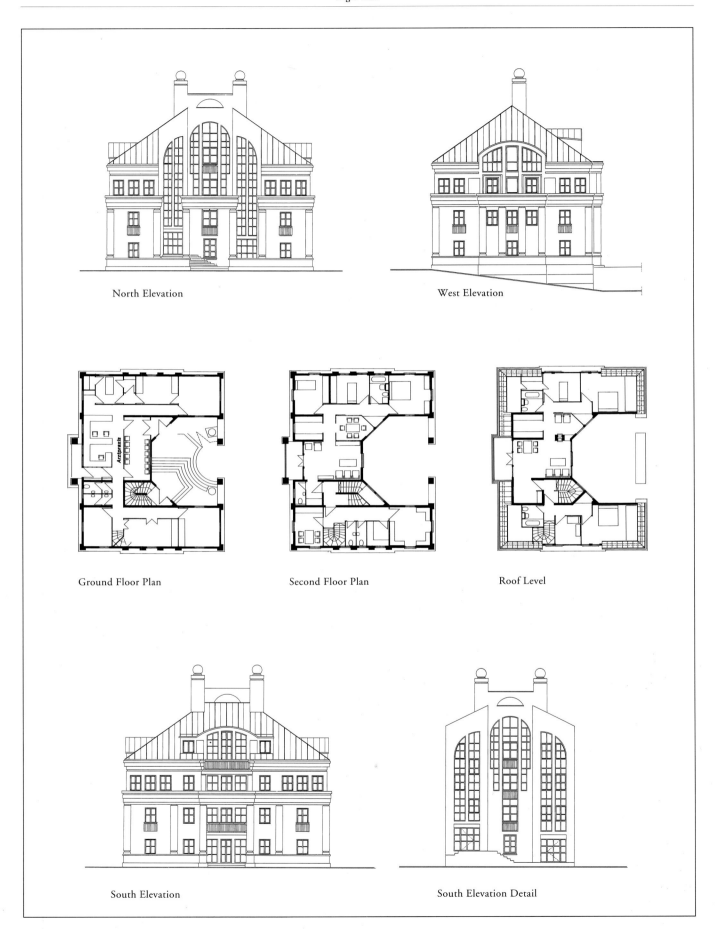

North Elevation

West Elevation

Ground Floor Plan

Second Floor Plan

Roof Level

South Elevation

South Elevation Detail

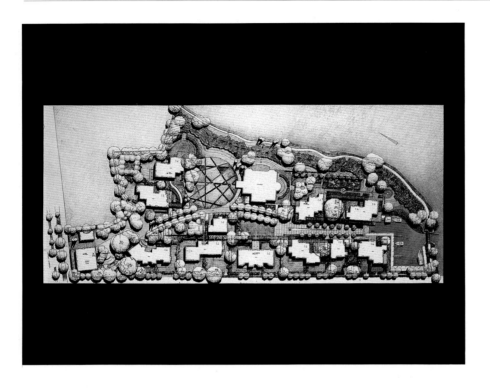

BERLINERSTRASSE HOUSING

Potsdam, Germany

A site for 75 luxury condominiums is situated southwest of Berlin at the gateway to Potsdam lying at the center of a network of pastoral views between nineteenth century neo-classical palaces and Baroque downtown Potsdam. An existing villa, which will be restored to late nineteenth century splendor, stands beside the Havel River at the edge of the site. Our task was to locate 12 individual villas in a manner to complement and frame the rather large existing villa, as well as relate to the delicate and more refined scale of romantic classical buildings by Schinkel and his colleague Persius, visible nearby. The buildings contain 3 to 10 units each and share contiguous underground parking.

The new villas, though comparable in scale to the existing house, establish a range of scales and connections to the landscape using pergolas, pavilions and roof gardens. The massing combines rational volumes and picturesque compositions, recalling especially memorable aspects of the "Potsdam Style." They use traditional, simply expressive materials — stone bases, stucco walls and tiles roofs — adding layers of glassy towers, bays and loggias to bring the fleeting hours of sunlight deep into the units.

The site plan is divided into three distinct areas: a cluster of villas at the entry arranged around open lawns; a formal landscaped court adjacent to the existing villa which is defined by arcades and symmetrical facades as well as a new canal-like marina leading to the Havel; and houses tight against it to frame a dramatic view of water and park land beyond. The units are a mix of small, medium and large types which balance the formality of neo-classical plans with twentieth century open plan interiors. A language of great rooms with bays and inglenooks creates a variety of special unit plans, yet encourages continuity in the elevations. Landscape treatment is derived from a similar idea of a set of pieces — pergolas, penthouses, and garden rooms — which connect the freestanding villas as well as recall their illustrious neighbors.

Project: Berlinerstrasse Housing
Size of Lot: 10,000 square meters
Size of Project: 75 luxury condominiums

Owner: Groth & Graalfs
Design Architect: Moore Ruble Yudell
Principal-in-Charge,
Principal Architect: John Ruble
Principal Architect: Charles Moore
Principal Architect: Buzz Yudell
Project Architect: Daniel Garness
Project Team: Curtis Woodhouse, Mary Beth Elliot, Mark Peacor, Marc Shoeplein, Roger Carvalheiro, John Taft, Craig Currie, Don Dimster
Associated Architect: Pysall Stahrenberg & Partner
Landscape Architect: Arge Müller Knippschild Wehberg
Color: Tina Beebe
Renderings: Al Forster
Project Liaison: Miller Stevens
Photography: Craig Currie, Moore Ruble Yudell Collection

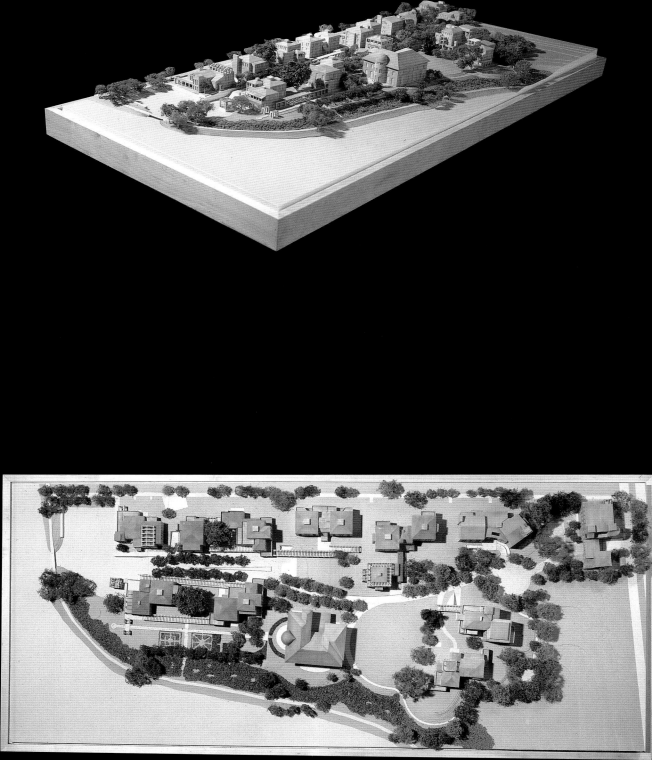

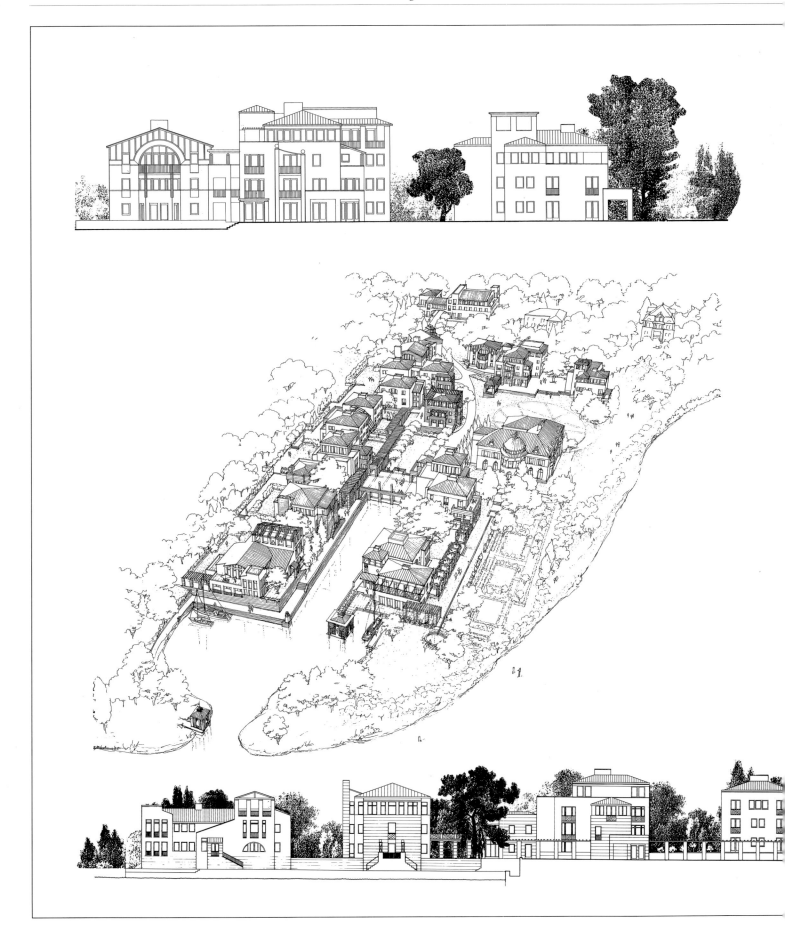

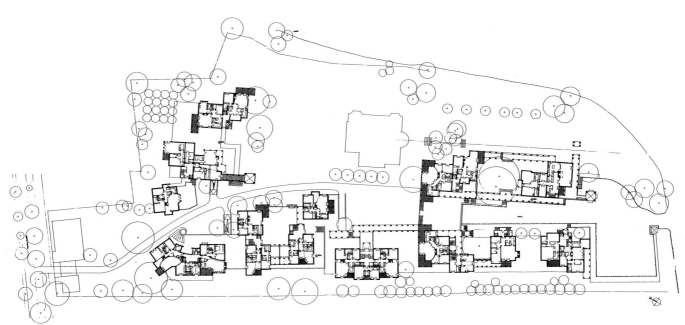

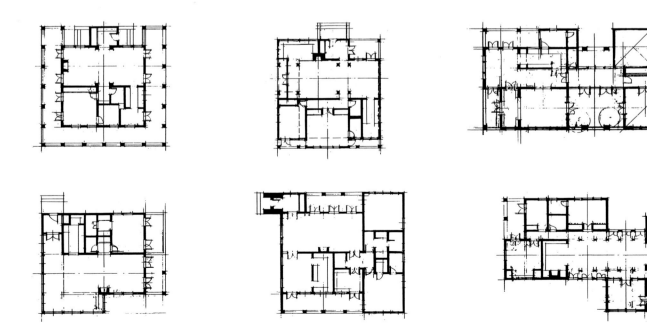

KIRCHSTEIGFELD MASTER PLAN

Potsdam, Germany

As a result of the intense growth initiated since the reunification of Germany, this field, located near historic Potsdam, is to be developed into a new town. The developer, in collaboration with the City of Potsdam, invited us to participate in a workshop for the master planning of the site. At the conclusion of the workshop, we were asked to collaborate with another participant, Rob Krier, for the further development of the master plan.

The site represents a microcosm of the issues of development in East Germany since reunification: to the west, a small village, 700 years old, overrun by the sudden burgeoning of traffic through to Berlin; to the north, the Neues Siedlung, reminder of the brutalism of post-war planning; to the south, the Autobahn, linking East Germany to the larger Germany.

On this 53 hectare site we were asked to propose a plan for a new town which will provide the full complement of civic, commercial and residential uses including 2,500–3,000 housing units, 160,000 square meters of commercial uses, two elementary schools, one high school, a sports center and public parks and services.

Our approach involved planning for a New Garden Village which is based on a neighborhood–oriented community that allows for choice and diversity within an integrated fabric. The open space network is carefully developed to create connections to the neighboring communities as well as a spectrum of spaces from community parks to intimate gardens. Housing typologies emphasize connection to identifiable private and communal spaces. They incorporate a range of densities and characters depending on their locations. Similarly, commercial typologies vary in configuration and relationship to other uses. The sense of neighborhood identity is enhanced both by the fabric of streets and open space and by the location of mixed-use services. As in the richest examples of urban life, the plan allows for architectural diversity and a harmonious urban fabric.

Project: Kirchsteigfeld Master Plan
Size of Lot: 53 hectares
Size of Project: 2,500–3,000 housing units plus 160,000 square meters of commercial, service and industrial spaces

Design Architect: Moore Ruble Yudell Principals-in-Charge,
Principal Architects: John Ruble, Buzz Yudell
Project Architect: Shuji Kurokawa
Phase I Team: Adrian J. Koffka, Mario Violich, James May O'Connor, Steve Gardner, Daniel Garness, Mary Beth Elliott, Louis Bretana, Adam Padua
Project Liaison: Miller Stevens
Competition: Project Architect: Mark Peacor; Competition Team: Cecily Young, Mario Violich, Curtis Woodhouse, Tony Tran, Richard Destin, John Taft, Craig Currie, Don Dimster, Celina Welch
Participating Firms: Augusto Romano Burelli; Eyl; Weitz; Würmle & Partner; Nielebock & Partner; Rob Krier and Partner; Moore Ruble Yudell; Krüger; Salzl; Vandreike; C. Schuberth
Renderings: Al Forster
Photography: Craig Currie, Moore Ruble Yudell Collection

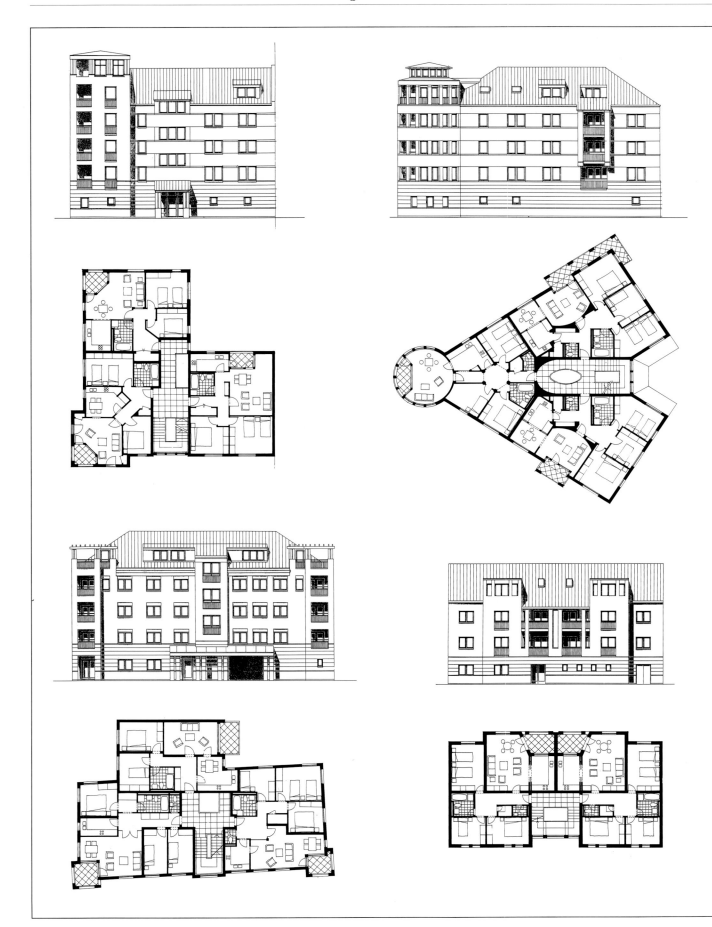

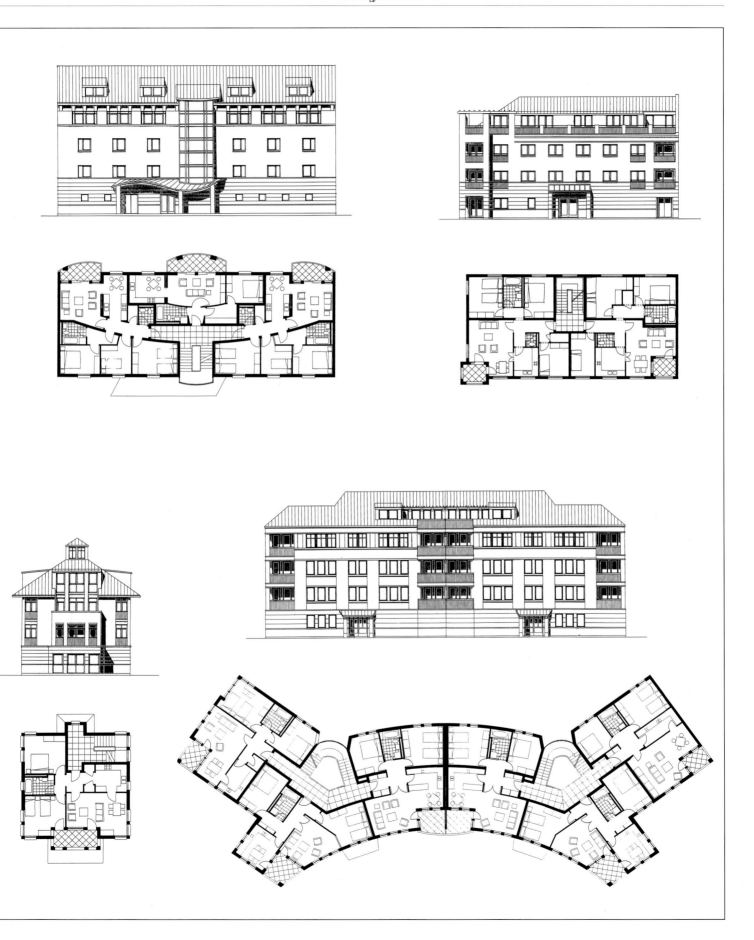

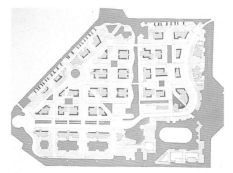

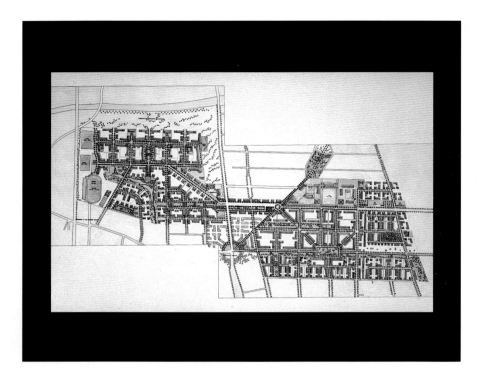

KAROW NORD MASTER PLAN
Berlin, Germany

The pressing need for housing in newly unified Berlin is creating occasions for re-examining the German tradition of "siedlungen" or large-scale housing developments.

One such project is our plan for a substantial expansion of the existing town of Karow, at the northeast edge of Berlin proper. The town is one of a string of communities surrounded by agricultural fields yet connected umbilically to the Autobahn which surrounds central Berlin. At the center of Karow is a small historic village: one street of simple agrarian buildings clustered around intimate courts.

Our task was to integrate 5,000 new housing units and requisite schools, playgrounds and shopping areas into this delicate context, deferring to the existing small scale character, while making a new identity for the necessarily denser new areas.

The site consists of two large, flat fields north of the historic village comprising 98 hectares. These fields flank the road to Berlin and are connected by a narrow parcel. Our scheme drew from the traditions of Garden Cities, growing out of the existing town pattern. The whole is organized by a network of green spaces, which will eventually weave through the town, with linear parks extending like agrarian fingers to the fields beyond.

The grading of scales eases the transition from the existing two-story town to new four-story housing blocks in the densest areas. The building types in this transition allow for a variety of public and private open space relationships: two-story "agrarian row houses" with individual yards on walk-streets; "Karow court" clusters of two and three stories, inspired by the example of the historic village center; three and four-story freestanding villas; and larger perimeter block buildings at the center.

The narrow connecting parcel between the two sites resulted in an important new public space, similar in shape to the historic village and complementary in use. This new main street is mixed-use, with housing over commercial space, which collects these and small civic uses into one cohesive space.

Project: Karow Nord Master Plan
Size of Lot: 98 hectares
Size of Project: 5,000 housing units plus 20,000 square meters of mixed-use and 180,000 square meters of institutional spaces

Master Planners: Moore Ruble Yudell
Principal-in-Charge,
Principal Architect: Buzz Yudell
Principal Architect: John Ruble
Project Architect: Daniel Garness
Project Coordinator: Miller Stevens
Project Team: Mark Peacor, Etchika Badzies, Adam Padua, Gearge Venini, Mary Beth Elliott, Curtis Woodhouse, Mario Violich, John Johnson, Wing Hon Ng, Craig Currie, Louis Bretana, Mark Grand, Niels Turnbull, Eric Hammerlund, Celina Welch
Landscape Planners: Arge Müller, Knippschild Wehberg
Principal-in-Charge: Cornelia Müler
Regional Planners: Freie Planungsgruppe Berlin; Gerard Schneider, Susanne Klar
Bebauungsplanners: Büro Obermeyer, J. Hoffmann
Renderings: Al Forster, Daniel Garness
Photography: Craig Currie, Moore Ruble Yudell Collection

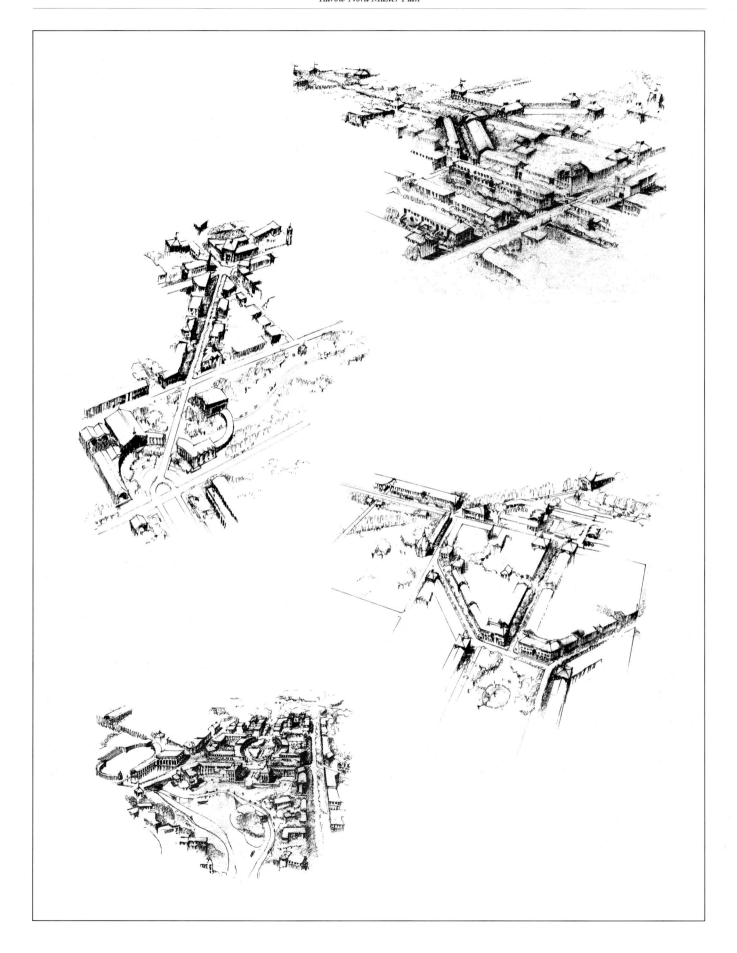

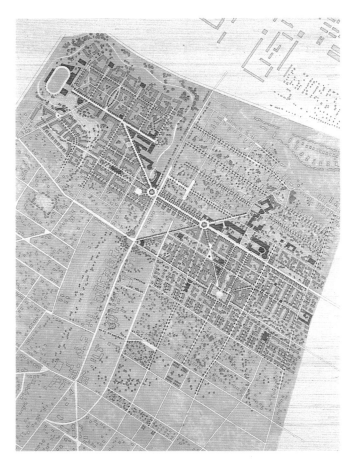

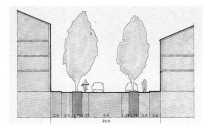

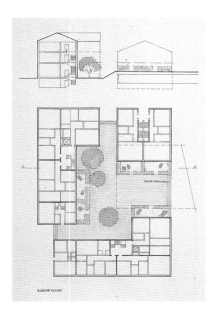

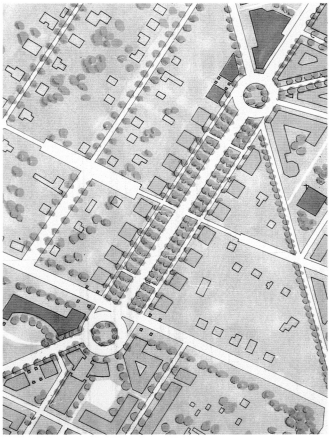

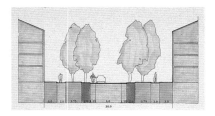

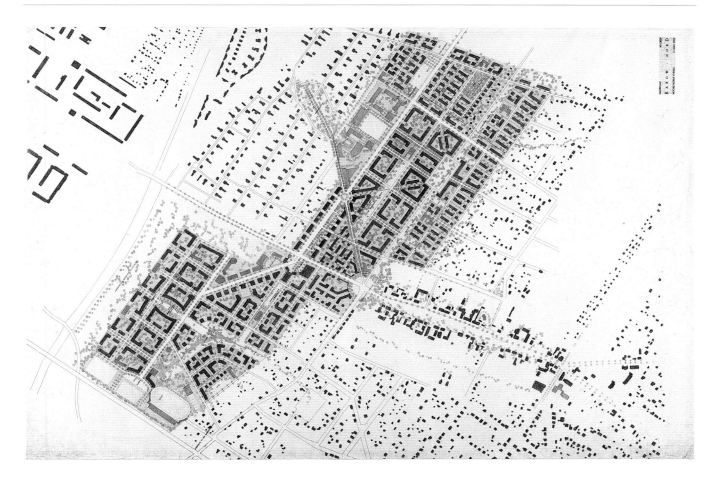

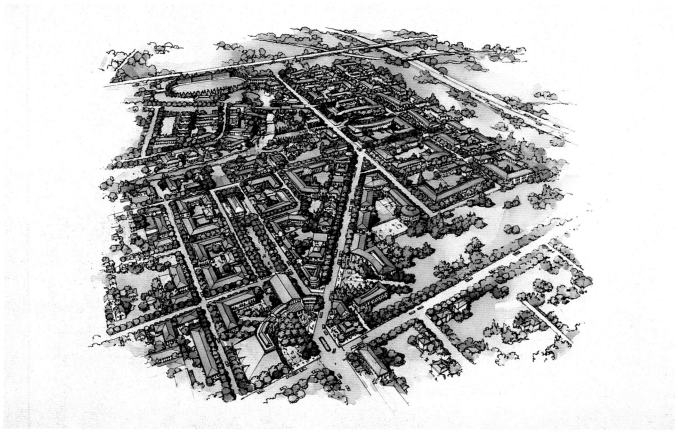

Biographies

Charles W. Moore

Education

Princeton University, doctor of philosophy degree received 1957
Princeton University, master of fine arts in architecture degree received 1956
University of Michigan, bachelor of architecture degree received 1947

Teaching Experience

O'Neill Ford Professor of architecture, School of Architecture, University of Texas at Austin, 1985 to present
Professor, University of California, Los Angeles, School of Architecture and Urban Planning, 1984 to present
Professor, Yale University School of Architecture, 1970 to 1975
Dean, Yale University School of Architecture, 1965 to 1970
Associate Professor, Chairman, University of California, Berkeley, department of architecture, 1959 to 1965
Associate Professor, Princeton University School of Architecture, 1957 to 1959
Assistant Professor of architecture, University of Utah, 1950 to 1952

Professional Experience

Principal, Moore Ruble Yudell, Santa Monica, California, 1977 to present
Principal, Moore Grover Harper/Centerbrook, Essex, Connecticut, 1974 to 1990
Principal, Moore/Anderson, Austin, Texas, 1992 to present
Associated with Urban Innovations Group (practice arm of UCLA School of Architecture), 1975 to 1991
Principal, Charles W. Moore Associates, Essex, Connecticut, 1970 to 1974
Principal, MLTW/Moore Turnbull, San Francisco, California, 1965 to 1970
Principal, Moore Lyndon Turnbull Whitaker (MLTW), 1962 to 1964
Clark and Beuttler, San Francisco, California, 1959 to 1962
Lieutenant, U. S. Army Corps of Engineers in the United States, Japan and Korea, 1952 to 1954
Worked in offices of Mario Corbett, Joseph Allen Stein, and Clark and Beuttler, San Francisco, California, 1947 to 1949

John Ruble

Education

University of California, Los Angeles, School of Architecture and Urban Planning, master of architecture degree received 1976
University of Virginia, bachelor of architecture degree received 1969

Teaching Experience

Lecturer, University of California, Los Angeles, School of Architecture and Urban Planning, 1981 to present
Visiting Lecturer, Cornell University, 1976
Teaching Associate, University of California, Los Angeles, School of Architecture and Urban Planning, 1975

Professional Experience

Principal, Moore Ruble Yudell, Santa Monica, California, 1977 to present
Consultant, Direct Energy Corporation, Irvine, California (solar heating and cooling development grant, U.S. Department of Energy), 1977 to 1978
Associated with Charles W. Moore, Los Angeles, 1976 to 1977
Project Manager, Urban Innovations Group, Los Angeles, 1976 to 1977
Associated with O. M. Ungers, Ithaca, New York, 1976
Designer, Uniplan, Princeton, New Jersey, 1971 to 1975
Urban Designer, Peace Corps, Tunisia Kasserine Bureau d'Urbanisme, Ministre de Tourisme et l'Amenagement du Territoire, 1969 to 1970

Buzz Yudell

Education

Yale School of Architecture, master of architecture degree received 1972
Yale College, bachelor of arts cum laude degree received 1969

Teaching Experience

Adjunct Professor, University of California, Los Angeles, School of Architecture and Urban Planning, 1977 to present
Visiting Critic, Technical University of Nova Scotia, Halifax School of Architecture, 1983
Visiting Critic, University of Texas at Austin, School of Architecture, 1981
Visiting Critic in architectural design, Yale School of Architecture, 1971 to 1976

Professional Experience

Principal, Moore Ruble Yudell, Santa Monica, California, 1977 to present
Designer, Project Manager, Charles Moore Architect, Los Angeles, California, 1976 to 1977
Project Manager, Urban Innovations Group, Los Angeles, California, 1976 to 1977
Principal, General Electric, New Haven, Connecticut, 1974 to 1976
Evans Wollen Architects, Hotchkiss, Connecticut (site office), 1973
Charles W. Moore Associates/Moore Grover Harper, Essex, Connecticut, 1972 to 1973

Moore Ruble Yudell Selected Awards & Distinctions

American Institute of Architects, Interiors Award, Nativity Catholic Church, 1993
Interior Award, Interiors Magazine, Nativity Catholic Church, 1992
Firm of the Year 1992, California Council American Institute of Architects
California Council, American Institute of Architects, Honor Award, 1992,

Yudell/Beebe House, Malibu, California

Sunset Magazine/American Institute of Architects Award, 1992, Yudell/Beebe House, Malibu, California

American Library Association/AIA Library Building Award, 1991, Humboldt Library

American Institute of Architects, Gold Medal for a lifetime of professional achievement, 1991, (Charles W. Moore)

American Wood Council, Honor Award, 1991—First Church of Christ, Scientist

American Institute of Architects/American Library Council Award, 1990—Humboldt Library

Los Angeles Chapter, American Institute of Architects, Honor Award, 1989—Humboldt Library

California Council, American Institute of Architects, Merit Award, 1989—Anawalt House

California Council, American Institute of Architects, Honor Award, 1988—Carousel Park

American Institute of Architects Honor Award, 1988—Tegel Harbor Housing

California Council, American Institute of Architects, Honor Award, 1988—Tegel Harbor Housing

Building a Better Future Honor Award, 1987 (State of California Department of Rehabilitation Architectural Design Awards Program)—Carousel Park

City of Santa Monica Mayor's Commendation, October 1987—Carousel Park

Excellence on the Waterfront Honor Award, Waterfront Center, 1987—Carousel Park

American Institute of ArchFirst Prize, City of Oceanside Civic Center Competition, 1986

American Institute of Architects Honor Award, 1984—St. Matthew's Church

California Council, American Institute of Architects, Merit Award, 1984—St. Matthew's Church

Los Angeles Chapter, American Institute of Architects, Merit Award, 1984—St. Matthew's Church

Architectural Record Houses of the Year, 1981—Rodes House

First Prize, Tegel Harbor International Design Competition, West Berlin 1980—Housing, Recreational and Cultural Center

Moore Ruble Yudell Selected Published Work

Moore Ruble Yudell, (1993) London: Academy Editions,

"Moore Ruble Yudell, 1979-1982," *Architecture and Urbanism*, August 1992

"University of Oregon Science Complex," *Arch*, March/April, 1992

"Nishiokamoto Housing," *Arch*, January/February, 1992

"Designers of the Year," *Interiors*, January, 1992—Nativity Catholic Church

"Earthly Delights, A California Design Couple's Country Idyll" (cover), *House Beautiful*, August, 1992

"Outdoor Rooms" (cover), *Elle Decor*, April/May, 1992

"University of Oregon Science Complex"(cover), *Architectural Record*, November, 1991

"Tegel Harbor Housing," *Arch*, May/ June, 1991

"Humboldt Bibliotek" (cover), *American Libraries*, April, 1991

"Collaborative Genius," "Angeleno Gothic," "Campus Medicine," *Architecture, March*, 1991

"Nativity Catholic Church" (cover), *Architectural Record*, February, 1991

"Bel Air Presbyterian Church" (cover), *American Organist*, February, 1991

"University of Oregon Science Complex" (cover), *Places*, Vol 7, No. 4, 1991

"Collaborative Genius," "Angeleno Gothic," "Campus Medicine," *Architecture*, March, 1991

"Malibu on their Minds" (cover), *House and Garden*, February, 1991

Moore Ruble Yudell—A Malibu Residence," *Architectural Digest*, February 1990—House on Point Dume

"Pride of Place," *Architectural Record*, January 1990—Humboldt Library

"Waterfront Housing at Once Exuberant and Classical," *Architecture*, May 1988—Tegel Harbor Housing

"Berlino 1988," *Housing,* May, 1988, Milano, Italy—Tegel Harbor,

'Housing That's Changing the Face of West Berlin," *The New York Times*, April 14, 1988—Tegel Harbor Housing

"Living by the Water" (cover), Progressive Architecture, October, 1987—Tegel Harbor Housing

"Moore Ruble Yudell—Remodeling a Spanish Colonial House in Beverly Hills" (cover), *Architectural Digest*, September, 1987—Pynoos House

"Charles Moore" (cover), *Interiors*, September, 1987—St. Matthew's Church, Church of the Nativity, Humboldt Library

"Rebuilding Berlin—Yet Again," *Time*, June, 15, 1987—Tegel Harbor Housing

"Das Pathos endet an der Haustür," *Der Spiegel*, June 1, 1987—Tegel Harbor Housing

"King Studio, Marine Street Residence." In *American Houses, by Philip Langdom. New York: Stewart, Tabori & Chang, 1987.*

"Perfection in Miniature", *House Beautiful*, February, 1987—King Studio

"St. Matthew's Church, Tegel Harbor Housing, Humboldt Library, San Juan Capistrano Library." *Charles Moore, Buildings and Projects 1949–986*, edited by Eugene J. Johnson. New York: Rizzoli, 1986—

"Overview of Recent Works," *Space Design*, November, 1986—Tegel Harbor, Plaza Las Fuentes, the Parador Hotel, St. Matthew's Church, San Antonio Art Institute, Kwee House

"Rodes House, Marine Street Residence." In *Freestyle*, by Tim Street-Porter, New York: Stewart, Tabori & Chang, 1986.

"Architecture—Moore Ruble Yudell," *Architectural Digest*, August, 1985—Kwee House

"Built on Religious, Regional Tradition, St. Matthew's Church," *Architecture*, May, 1984, Washington, D.C.

"Design by Congregation," *Architectural Record*, February 1984—St. Matthew's Church

"St. Matthew's Parish Church," *Architecture & Urbanism*, January, 1984, Tokyo 1981

"Tegel Harbor Housing." In *Erste Projekte, Internationale Bauausstellung Berlin 1984*. Berlin, 1981.

"A Church is Not a Home," *Newsweek*, March, 1983—St. Matthew's Church

"Charles Moore: Recent Projects," *Architectural Review*, August, 1981, London

"Houses of the Year," *Architectural Record*, May, 1981—Rodes House

"New American Architecture 1981," *Architecture & Urbanism*, Tokyo, 1981

"Charles Moore and Company," *Global Architecture,* No. 7, Tokyo, 1980

Notes from the Architects

We wish to express our appreciation for the energetic efforts of the publishers, editors and designers of this volume. The task of shaping a varied body of work, represented by words, drawings and photographs into a coherent and meaningful whole is a daunting challenge. Here the work has been especially complex because of parallel publications in English and Spanish. Thoughtful and committed collaboration between several organizations has been essential to the success of this book. We wish to thank Rockport Publishers and their President Stanley Patey and

their Senior Editor Rosalie Grattaroti for their support of architecture and commitment to the highest standards of publication and design. Editors and Designers Oscar Riera Ojeda and Lucas Guerra of Connexus Visual Communication have brought a lucid vision of how to structure and present the material of the book.

They have supplied energy and insight in abundance from the inception of the project. John Ray Hoke and the American Institute of Architects have been enthusiastic and supportive of the publication. We are delighted that the Spanish publisher ASPPAN and the Argentine Publisher CP 67 have collaborated on Spanish editions. Guillermo and Hugo Kliczkowski have been instrumental in this initiative. James Mary O'Connor, one of our Senior Project Architects has been persevering and enthusiastic as he has worked with Oscar Riera Ojeda to see this book realized. Finally, the projects and ideas represented here are all the result of intense collaboration with our office, our clients, and the communities in which we have worked. Their energy, ideas and support have been essential to any success we have had in the making of places.